SYBARIS

AND OTHER HOMES.

BY

EDWARD E. HALE.

BOSTON:
FIELDS, OSGOOD, & CO.
1869.

University Press: Welch, Bigelow, & Co.,
Cambridge.

DEDICATION.

I DEDICATE this book to the

SUFFOLK UNION FOR CHRISTIAN WORK.

At the meeting which formed that Society the provision for better homes in cities was publicly declared to be the first work of Christian reform. At every meeting since some person has enforced the same necessity.

EDWARD E. HALE.

SOUTH CONGREGATIONAL CHURCH, BOSTON,
September 18, 1869.

PREFACE.

The reader will see that the papers in this book have a single object, whether cast in the form of fiction, or whether statistical narratives of fact. If I should classify them as the papers were classified in an earlier volume of this little series, the account of Naguadavick is the account of what ought to be; the account of Vineland is the account of what is; and the account of Boston is the account of what ought not to be. In the narrative of Sybaris the reader will find something of "if," something of "yes," something of "perhaps"; some possibility, much fact, and some exaggeration.

I have, perhaps, a right to explain the earnestness with which I try to enforce the necessity of better homes for laboring men by stating a single circumstance in my own history. For nearly twenty-five years I have been constantly engaged in the Christian ministry. About half that time was spent in Worcester, Massachusetts; about half of it in Boston. When I went to Worcester it was a town of about eight thousand people; when I left it, it had three times that number. Boston is a crowded town of a quarter-million inhabitants. It is impossible for me not to notice, in every hour of my life, the contrast between the homes of the working people in these two places. I might almost say that there is no other difference of importance between the social opportunities of the two places. They are not far apart; both are active places of business, employing in about equal proportions people of enterprise and energy, in the varied work of manufacture, commerce, and transportation. But in one of these places almost every man can own his house, and half the men do. In the other hardly any man can own his house, and half the people are crowded into quarters where no man should be compelled to live.

To watch over and improve the charities of any town is the special duty of the Christian ministry in it, — to feed its hungry and clothe its naked, to open the eyes of its blind and the ears of its deaf, to make its lame walk, to cleanse its lepers, and to preach good tidings to its poor. Will the reader imagine to himself the position of the man engaged in that duty, when he finds his sick in such tenements as they must live in in our present system, — his blind, for instance, born so, perhaps, in rooms with no window, and all his poor in such homes that the only truly good tidings are tidings which send them away from him? Where a considerable part of the people live in such homes our best devised charities, either for moral culture or physical relief, work at terrible odds. Your

City Missions, your Ministry at Large, your Industrial Aid Society, or your Overseers of the Poor are all working against the steady dead weight which, as we all know, presses down and holds down the man who is in an unhealthy or unhappy home.

The contrast in my own life between life in a small manufacturing and commercial town and life in a large one makes me feel the bitterness of these odds the more. I am sure that the suffering thus involved is unnecessary, as I am sure the labor which tries to relieve its symptoms must be in large measure thrown away. With an intense personal interest, therefore, have I attempted to show in this book how these evils may be remedied.

I do not know but Colonel Ingham's suggestions as to his imagined Sybaris may be thought too roseate and ideal for our Western longitudes. They have been already published in the Atlantic Monthly, and, in his absence in Siberia, I have been once and again favored with criticisms upon them. It is but fair to him to say, that, so far as the paper refers to ancient Sybaris or Thurii, it is a very careful study of the best authorities regarding that interesting state, — a study which I wish might be pushed further by somebody. And I incorporate the paper in this volume because it seems to me that we have a great deal to learn from the ancient cities and from their methods of government, were it only the great lesson of the value of training in administration.

There is a very odd habit of speech about republican government, which, like most careless habits of speech, hurts our practice. When the theory of a republic is discussed, everybody says that it worked admirably in cities of compact territory, but that it failed when it had to be extended over wider regions. This is really a commonplace in the old-fashioned sturdy books on political institutions. But when you come to talk politics with practical people to-day, the chances are nine in ten that they say, "Ah, republican institutions are admirable for the country at large; they work perfectly for a scattered population; but when you come to compact cities you want something very different. Must have one head there, one head there," &c., &c., &c. Now certainly this is very odd, that just as we have all learned to repeat one of these lessons from old Greek and Roman history, illustrated in the history of Greek and Roman colonies, we should all have to turn round and say exactly the other thing. Is it not probable that there is some misunderstanding?

I believe that a careful study of the history of the Greek and Roman cities shows that their success is largely due to their attention to the science of administration. The men who discharged specific functions were trained to those functions, and knew how to discharge them. In the Roman cities no man could be a candidate for the higher grades of service, unless he had served so manv years in the lower. Any old Roman, asked to vote in our city elections, would take it for granted that no man could be an alderman who had not been a common-council-man for a certain number of years, nor a mayor unless he had been an alderman for a certain number. In Athens they were even more careful, and all officers were as distinctly trained to their duties as with us civil engineers are or architects. What followed was, that when the right man got into place, there was a reasonable probability that he stayed in.

In our elective city governments, on the other hand, with a great deal of good feeling and a great deal of public spirit, we find uncertainty, hurry sometimes, and delay in others, frequent changes in system, shyness about responsibility, and, in consequence, a great deal of discomfort and grumbling. I once asked a very able and pure man, then Mayor of Boston, why the city did not undertake a certain policy, which seemed important. "How should I know?" said he, with a sigh. "I was chosen to this place eight months ago, with no experience in city affairs. If I am chosen again in December, I may have heart to start on some such proposal as you name. But really, the first year of a man's service as Mayor must be given to learning where he stands." This is perfectly true.

Now, at the end of the first year who determines whether such a man shall or shall not go on? Almost always, five hundred men, united, can settle that thing one way or another. If he have wounded the feelings of the policemen, — if he have made a change in the management of the fire companies, — if in any way he have crossed the track of any compact organization, he is put out and some other new man is put in, for his apprenticeship. I do not believe that this system of neophyte mayors is necessary. And I believe that whenever the public is roused to study it, it will be changed.

It does not make so much difference in Boston, however, because the Mayor has no great power, after all. He is not much more than a chairman of selectmen. The same difficulty, as it seems to me, comes in in the choice of the aldermen, who have, collectively, some power. I read a great deal of insulting language and bitter sneering about aldermen. I suppose there are bad aldermen, as I know there are bad ministers, bad painters, and bad bootmakers. But, in my experience, the aldermen with whom I have had to confer on the affairs of the city have been hard-working, upright, intelligent, public-spirited men, doing a great deal of work, for which they got no pay and no thanks; and doing it, under our lumbering system, very well. But they were all doing it by instinct, and not after training. They had happened upon the situation which made them a directory of twelve, governing, in nice details of administration, a city of a quarter-million people. They had never been trained in advance to do that duty. And, by the time they had learned it, in presence of the enemy, they were heartily sick of it, and were glad to resign.

It seems to me, that as long as we govern cities in that way, we shall have bad horse-cars, bad tenement-houses, bad streets, bad theatres, bad liquor-shops, and a great many other bad things, which, in a city where administration was a science, and no man chosen to office until he had been trained to it, Colonel Ingham did not find in Sybaris.

I observe that the newspapers are a good deal exercised when a committee of the city government, or when any city officers, go to study the systems of some other cities. For my part, I wish they went a great deal oftener than they do, and studied such systems a great deal more. I believe the city of Boston could make no wiser expenditure than it would make in sending to Europe, once in five years, an intelligent officer from each great department to study French, English, German, Italian, and Russian administration of streets; of hackney-coaches, omnibuses, and railroad stations; of prisons, of the detective and general police; of health; of markets, and of education. There is hardly a large city in the civilized world which has not some hints of value which it could give to every other city.

Colonel Ingham has received many protests against the arbitrary and unprincipled action of the government of Sybaris in compelling marriage among its people. He had already made his own protest, as he could, in his journal. Nor would he wish to be understood as desiring to enforce anywhere statutes so tyrannical. But, as I understand him, he is convinced, by what he has seen in Sybaris and in the rest of the world, that every artificial obstacle to marriage is so much multiplication of all other evil in the world, and whether that obstacle come in the form of fashion, of custom, of sentiment, of gossip, of political economy, or of law, it is to be deprecated and set aside.

I may add that I do not know why such views have not a larger place than they have in the current discussions of female suffrage. The married woman and the married man being one, she now has suffrage. How would it answer to withdraw suffrage from the unmarried men? This would put them on an equality with the unmarried women; and there would be a possibility, if they are troubled by the loss, of their regaining the privilege.

But I will not, in a preface, discuss the details of any of the experiments in city administration here suggested. My chief wish is accomplished, if I can call attention to the delicacy and difficulty of these questions, and to the necessity of studying them with scientific and conscientious precision. When our best men study the details of local administration with the care with which Themistocles, Aristides, and Pericles studied them in Athens, — with which Metellus, the Catos, Pompey the Great, and Julius Cæsar were willing to study them in Rome, — we shall find, as I believe, no difficulty in the republican government of cities.

The shorter essays in this book are devoted to the single subject of the homes of laborers at work in large cities, and, as I trust, require no further explanation.

As the last sheets of this book leave my hands, the watchful kindness of a friend enables me to add the last word regarding Sybaris.

Under the title "De Paris a Sybaris," (Paris: A. Lemerre, 1868,) M. Léon Palustre de Montifaut publishes his studies of art and literature in Rome and Southern Italy. And here is his record of what he saw of Sybaris. He speaks first of Cassano, the last Italian town which looks down upon the valley of ancient Sybaris.

"Cassano, with its beautiful gardens, its tranquil aspect, and its gray mountains, reminds one of the ancient Sichem. It has its freshness and its poetry, if it has not the same reminiscences.

"Still, I hastened my departure, for I was eager to cross before night those broad and marshy expanses over which the eye travelled without an obstacle, — a vast semicircle cut into the thickness of the Apennine, or fertile intervals left by the sea.

"And what was I going to see? Not so much as a ruin, — an uncertain region over which lay loose the voluptuous name of Sybaris. And I had made a long journey.. I had undergone incredible fatigue to give myself this empty satisfaction. How the inhabitants of this easy city would have laughed at me! They could not understand, says Athenæus, why one should quit his country. For themselves they gloried in growing old where they first saw the light. Yet this people practised the broadest hospitality, and, contrary to the policy of most of the Greek states, they readily admitted the colonists of other nations to the rank of citizens. May not this liberal spirit and the astonishing fertility of the soil explain the prosperity of this prosperous town, which is so strangely kept in obscurity by all antiquity? Varro tells us that wheat produced a hundred-fold on the whole territory of Sybaris. At the present time the uplands produce the richest harvests."

And this, I am sorry to say, is the only contribution to the history or topography of Sybaris made since the date of Mr. Ingham's voyage. Mons. Montifaut, alas like all the others! hurried across the upland six miles back from the sea. It is as if a traveller from Providence, coming up to Readville, should cross to Watertown and Waltham, and then, going through the Notch of the White Mountains to Montreal, should publish his observations on Boston.

And these notes, alas, as late as 1867, are dated like Colonel Ingham's, on the 1st of April!

CONTENTS.

MY VISIT TO SYBARIS.

FROM REV. FREDERIC INGHAM'S PAPERS.

It is a great while since I first took an interest in Sybaris. Sybarites have a bad name. But before I had heard of them anywhere else, I had painfully looked out the words in the three or four precious anecdotes about Sybaris in the old Greek Reader; and I had made up my boy's mind about the Sybarites. When I came to know the name they had got elsewhere, I could not but say that the world had been very unjust to them!

O dear! I can see it now, — the old Latin schoolroom, where we used to sit, and hammer over that Greek, after the small boys had gone. They went at eleven; we — because we were twelve or more — stayed till twelve. From eleven to twelve we sat, with only those small boys who had been "kept" for their sins, and Mr. Dillaway. The room was long and narrow; how long and how narrow you may see, if you will go and examine M. Duchesne's model of "Boston as it was," and pay twenty-five cents to the Richmond schools. For all this is of the past; and in the same spot in space where once a month the Examiner Club now meets at Parker's, and discusses the difference between religion and superstition, the folly of copyright, and the origin of things, the boys who did not then belong to the Examiner Club, say Fox and Clarke and Furness and Waldo Emerson, thumbed their Græca Minora or their Greek Readers in "Boston as it was," and learned the truth about Sybaris! A long, narrow room, I say, whose walls, when I knew them first, were of that tawny orange wash which is appropriated to kitchens. But, by a master stroke of Mr. Dillaway's, these walls were made lilac or purple one summer vacation. We sat, to recite, on long settees, pea-green in color, which would teeter slightly on the well-worn floor. There, for an hour daily, while brighter boys than I recited, I sat an hour musing, looking at the immense Jacobs's Greek Reader, and waiting my turn to come. If you did not look off your book much, no harm came to you. So, in the hour, you got fifty-three minutes and a few odd seconds of day-dream, for six minutes and two thirds of reciting, unless, which was unusual, some fellow above you broke down, and a question, passed along of a sudden, recalled you to modern life. I have been sitting on that old green settee, and at the same time riding on horseback in Virginia, through an open wooded country, with one of Lord Fairfax's grandsons and two pretty cousins of his, and a fallow deer has just appeared in the distance, when, by the failure of Hutchinson or Wheeler, just above me, poor Mr. Dillaway has had to ask me, "Ingham, what verbs omit the reduplication?" Talk of war! Where is versatility, otherwise called presence of mind, so needed as in recitation at a public school?

Well, there, I say, I made acquaintance with Sybaris. Nay, strictly speaking, my first visits to Sybaris were made there and then. What the Greek Reader tells of Sybaris is in three or four anecdotes, woven into that strange, incoherent patchwork of "Geography." In that place are patched together a statement of Strabo and one of Athenæus about two things in Sybaris which may have belonged some eight hundred years apart. But what of that to a school-boy! Will your descendants, dear reader, in the year 3579 A. D., be much troubled, if, in the English Reader of their day, Queen Victoria shall be made to drink Spartan black broth with William the Conqueror out of a conch-shell in New Zealand?

With regard to Sybaris, then, the old Jacobs's Greek Reader tells the following stories: "The Sybarites were distinguished for luxury. They did not permit the trades which made a loud noise, such as those of brass-workers, carpenters, and the like, to be carried on in the heart of the city, so that their sleep might be wholly undisturbed by noise. . . . . And a Sybarite who had gone to Lacedæmon, and had been invited to the public meal, after he had sat on their wooden benches and partaken of their fare, said that he had been astonished at the fearlessness of the Lacedæmonians when he knew it only by report; but now that he had seen them, he thought that they did not excel other men, for he thought that any brave man had much rather die than be obliged to live such a life as they did." Then there is another story, among the "miscellaneous anecdotes," of a Sybarite who was asked if he had slept well. He said, No, that he believed he had a crumpled rose-leaf under him in the night. And there is yet another, of one of them who said that it made his back ache to see another man digging.

I have asked Polly, as I write, to look in Mark Lemon's Jest-Book for these stories. They are not in the index there. But I dare say they are in Cotton Mather and Jeremy Taylor. Any way, they are bits of very cheap Greek. Now it is on such stories that the reputation of the Sybarites in modern times appears to depend.

Now look at them. This Sybarite at Sparta said, that in war death was often easier than the hardships of life. Well, is not that true? Have not thousands of brave men said it? When the English and French got themselves established on the wrong side of Sebastopol, what did that engineer officer of the French say to somebody who came to inspect his works? He was talking of St. Arnaud, their first commander. "Cunning dog," said he, "he went and died." Death was easier than life. But nobody ever said he was a coward or effeminate because he said this. Why, if our purpose would permit an excursus of two hundred pages here, on this theme, we would defer Sybaris to the 1st of April, 1870, while we illustrated the Sybarite's manly epigram, which these stupid Spartans could only gape at, but could not understand.

Then take the rose-leaf story. Suppose by good luck you were breakfasting with General Grant, or Pelissier, or the Duke of Wellington. Suppose you said, "I hope you slept well," and the great soldier said, "No, I did not; I think a rose-leaf must have stood up edgewise under me." Would you go off and say in your book of travels that the Americans, or the French, or the English are all effeminate pleasure-seekers, because one of them made this nice little joke? Would you like to have the name "American" go down to all time, defined as Webster * defines Sybarite?

A-MĔR'I-CAN, *n.* [Fr. *Américain,* Lat. *Americanus,* from Lat. *America,* a continent noted for the effeminacy and voluptuousness of its inhabitants.] A person devoted to luxury and pleasure.

Should you think that was quite fair for your great-grandson's grandson's descendant in the twenty-seventh remove to read, who is going to be instructed about Queen Victoria and William the Conqueror?

Worst of all, and most frequently quoted, is the story of the coppersmiths. The Sybarites, it is said, ordered that the coppersmiths and brass-founders should all reside in one part of the city, and bang their re-

* I am writing in Westerly's snuggery, and in Providence they believe in Webster's Dictionary. I dare say it is worse in Worcester's. A good many things are.

spective metals where the neighbors had voluntarily chosen to listen to banging. What if they did? Does not every manufacturing city practically do the same thing? What did Nicholas Tillinghast use to say to the boys and girls at Bridgewater? "The tendency of cities is to resolve themselves into order."

Is not Wall Street at this hour a street of bankers? Is not the Boston Pearl Street a street of leather men? Is not the bridge at Florence given over to jewellers? Was not my valise, there, bought in Rome at the street of trunk-makers? Do not all booksellers like to huddle together as long as they can? And when Ticknor and Fields move a few inches from Washington Street to Tremont Street, do not Russell and Bates, and Childs and Jenks, and De Vries and Ibarra, follow them as soon as the shops can be got ready?

"But it is the motive," pipes up the old gray ghost of propriety, who started this abuse of the Sybarites in some stupid Spartan black-broth shop (English that for *café*), two thousand two hundred and twenty-two years ago, — which ghost I am now belaboring, — "it is the motive. The Sybarites moved the brass-founders, because they wanted to sleep after the brass-founders got up in the morning." What if they did, you old rat in the arras? Is there any law, human or divine, which says that at one and the same hour all men shall rise from bed in this world? My excellent milkman, Mr. Whit, rises from bed daily at two o'clock. If he does not, my family, including Matthew, Mark,

Luke, John, and Acts, will not have their fresh milk at 7.37, at which time we breakfast or pretend to. But because he rises at two, must we all rise at two, and sit wretchedly whining on our respective camp-stools, waiting for Mr. Whit to arrive with the grateful beverage? Many is the time, when I have been watching with a sick child at five in a summer morning, when the little fellow had just dropped into a grateful morning doze, that I have listened and waited, dreading the arrival of the Providence morning express. For I knew that, a mile and a half out of Boston, the engine would begin to blow its shrill whistle, for the purpose, I believe, of calling the Boston station-men to their duty. Three or four minutes of that *skre-e-e-e* must there be, as that train swept by our end of the town. And hoping and wishing never did any good; the train would come, and the child would wake. Is not that a magnificent power for one engine-man to have over the morning rest of fifty thousand sleeping people, because you, old Spartan croaker, who can't sleep easy underground it seems, want to have everybody waked up at the same hour in the morning? When I hear that whistle, and the fifty other whistles of the factories that have since followed its wayward and unlicensed example, I have wished more than once that we had in Boston a little more of the firm government of Sybaris.

For if, as it would appear from these instances, Sybaris were a city which grew to wealth and strength by the recognition of the personal rights of each individual in the state, — if Sybaris were a republic, where the individual was respected, had his rights, and was not left to the average chances of the majority of men, — then Sybaris had found out something which no modern city has found out, and which it is a pity we have all forgotten.

I do not say that I went through all this speculation at the Latin school. I got no further there than to see that the Sybarites had got a very bad name, and that the causes did not appear in the Greek Reader. I supposed there were causes somewhere, which it was not proper to put into the Greek Reader. Perhaps there were. But if there were, I have never found them since, — not being indeed very well acquainted with the lines of reading in which those who wanted to find them should look for them.

WHAT I did find of Sybaris, when I could read Greek rather more easily, and could get access to some decent atlases, was briefly this.

Well forward in the hollow of the arched foot of the boot of Italy, two little rivers run into the Gulf of Tarentum. One was once named Crathis, one was named Sybaris. Here stood the ancient city of Sybaris, founded about the time of Romulus or Numa Pompilius, by a colony from Greece. For two hundred years and more, — almost as long, dear Atlantic, as your beloved Boston has subsisted, — Sybaris flourished, and was the Rome of that region, ruling it from sea to sea.

It was the capital of four states, — a sort of New England, if you will observe, — and could send three hundred thousand armed men into the field, more, I will observe in passing, than New England has, as yet, ever had occasion to send at one moment. The walls of the city were six miles in circumference, while the suburbs covered the banks of the Crathis for a space of seven miles. At last the neighboring state of Crotona, under the lead of Milon the Athlete (he of the calf and ox and split log), the Heenan or John Morrissey of his day, vanquished the more refined Sybarites, turned the waters of the Crathis upon their prosperous city, and destroyed it. But the Sybarites had had that thing happen too often to be discouraged. Five times, say the historians, had Sybaris been destroyed, and five times they built it up again. This time the Athenians sent ten vessels, with men to help them, under Lampon and Xenocritus. And they, with those who stood by the wreck, gave their new city the name of Thurii. Among the new colonists were Herodotus, and Lysias the orator, who was then a boy. The spirit that had given Sybaris its comfort and its immense population appeared in the legislation of the new state. It received its laws from CHARONDAS, one of the noblest legislators of the world. Study these laws and you will see that in the young Sybaris the individual had his rights, which the public preserved for him, though he were wholly in a minority. There is an evident determination that a man shall live while he lives, and that, too, in no sensual interpretation of the words.

Of the laws made by Charondas for the new Sybaris a few are preserved.

1. A calumniator was marched round the city in disgrace, crowned with tamarisk. "In consequence," says the Scholiast, "they all left the city." O for such a result, from whatever legislation, in our modern Pedlingtons, great or little!

2. All persons were forbidden to associate with the bad.

3. "He made another law, better than these, and neglected by the older legislators. For he enacted that all the sons of the citizens should be instructed in letters, the city paying the salaries of the teachers. For he held that the poor, not being able to pay their teachers from their own property, would be deprived of the most valuable discipline." There is FREE EDUCATION for you, two thousand and seventy-six years before the date of your first Massachusetts free school; and the theory of free education completely stated.

4. Deserters or cowards in battle had to sit in women's dresses in the Forum three days.

5. With regard to the amendment of laws, any man or woman who moved one did it with a noose round his neck, and was hanged if the people refused it. Only three laws were ever amended, therefore, all

which are recorded in the history. Observe that the women might move amendments, — and think of the simplicity of legislation!

6. The law provided for cash payments, and the government gave no protection for those who sold on credit.

7. Their communication with other nations was perfectly free.

I might give more instances. I should like to tell some of the curious stories which illustrate this simple legislation. Poor Charondas himself fell a victim to it. One of the laws provided that no man should wear a sword into the public assembly. No Cromwells there! Unfortunately, by accident, Charondas wore his own there one day. Brave fellow! when the fault was pointed out, he killed himself with it.

Now, do you wonder that a city, where there were no calumniators, no long credit, no bills at the grocers, no fighting at town-meetings, no amendments to the laws, no intentional and open association with profligates, and where everybody was educated by the state to letters, proved a comfortable place to live in? It is of the old Sybaris that the coppersmith and the rose-leaf stories are told; and it was the new Sybaris that made the laws. But do you not see that there is one spirit in the whole? Here was a nation which believed that the highest work of a nation was to train its people. It did not believe in fight, like Milon or Heenan or the old Spartans; it did not believe in legislation, like Massachusetts and New York; it did not believe in commerce, like Carthage and England. It believed in men and women. It respected men and women. It educated men and women. It gave their rights to men and women. And so the Spartans called them effeminate. And the Greek Reader made fun of them. But perhaps the people who lived there were indifferent to the opinions of the Spartans and of the Greek Reader. Herodotus lived there till he died; wrote his history there, among other things. Lysias, the orator, took part in the administration. It is not from them, you may be sure, that you get the anecdotes which ridicule the old city of Sybaris!

You and I would probably be satisfied with such company as that of Herodotus and Charondas and Lysias. So we hunt the history down to see if there may be lodgings to let there this summer, but only to find that it all pales out in the ignorance of our modern days. The name gets changed into Lupiæ; but there it turns out that Pausanias made a "strange mistake," and should have written Copia, — which was perhaps Cossa, or sometimes Cosa. Pyrrhus appears, and Hadrian rebuilds something, and the "Oltramontani," whoever they may have been, ravage it, and finally the Saracens fire and sack it; and so, in the latest Italian itinerary you can find, there is no post-road goes near it, only a *strada rotabile* (wheel-track) upon the hills; and, alas! even the *rotabile* gives way at last, and all the map will own to is a *strada pedonale*, or foot-path. But the map is of the less consequence, when you find that the man who edited it had no later dates than the beginning of the last century, when the family of Serra had transferred the title to Sybaris to a Genoese family without a name, who received from it forty thousand ducats yearly, and would have received more, if their agents had been more faithful. There the place fades out of history, and you find in your Swinburne, "that the locality has *never* been thoroughly examined"; in your Smith's Dictionary, that "the whole subject is very obscure, and a careful examination still much needed"; in the Cyclopædia, that the site of Sybaris is lost. Craven saw the rivers Crathis and Sybaris. He seems not to have seen the wall of Sybaris, which he supposed to be under water. He does say of Cassano, the nearest town he came to, that "no other spot can boast of such advantages." In short, no man living who has written any book about it dares say that anybody has looked upon the certain site of Sybaris for more than a hundred years.* If a man wanted to write a mythical story, where could he find a better scene?

* The reader who cares to follow the detail is referred to Diodorus Siculus, XII. 9 et seq.; Strabo, VI.; Ælian, V. H. 9, c. 24; Athenæus, XII. 518-520; Plutarch in Pelopidas; Herodotus, V. and VI. Compare Laurent's Geographical Notes, and Wheeler and Gaisford; Pliny, III. 15, VII. 22, XVI. 33, VIII. 64, XXXI. 9, 10; Aristotle, Polit. IV. 12, V. 3; Heyne's Opuscula, II. 74; Bentley's Phalaris, 367; Solinus, 2, § 10, "luxuries grossly exaggerated"; Scymnus, 337-360; Aristophanes, Vesp. 1427, 1436; Lycophron, Alex. 1079; Pausanias at Lupias; Polybius, Gen. Hist. II. 3, on the confederation of

Now is not this a very remarkable thing? Here was a city, which, under its two names of Sybaris or of Thurii, was for centuries the regnant city of all that part of the world. It could call into the field three hundred thousand men, — an army enough larger than Athens ever furnished, or Sparta. It was a far more populous and powerful state than ever Athens was, or Sparta, or the whole of Hellas. It invented and carried into effect free popular education, — a gift to the administration of free government larger than ever Rome rendered. It received and honored Charondas, the great practical legislator, from whose laws no man shall say how much has trickled down into the Code Napoleon or the Revised Statutes of New York, through the humble studies of the Roman jurists. It maintained in peace, prosperity, happiness, and, as its maligners say, in comfort, an immense population. If they had not been as comfortable as they were, — if a tenth part of them had received alms every year, and a tenth part were flogged in the public schools every year, and one in forty had been sent to prison every year, as in the happy city which pub-

Sybaris, Kroton, and Kaulonia, — "a perplexing statement," says Grote, "showing that he must have conceived the history of Sybaris in a very different form from that in which it is commonly represented"; third volume of De Non, who disagrees with Magnan as to the site of Sybaris, and says the sea-shore is uninhabitable! Tuccagni Orlandini, Vol. XI., Supplement, p. 294; besides the dictionaries and books of travels, including Murray. I have availed myself, without other reference, of most of these authorities.

lishes these humble studies, — then Sybaris, perhaps, would never have got its bad name for luxury. Such a city lived, flourished, ruled, for hundreds of years. Of such a city all that you know now with certainty is, that its coin is "the most beautifully finished in the cabinets of ancient coinage"; and that no traveller pretends to be sure that he has been to the site of it for more than a hundred years. That speaks well for your nineteenth century.

Now the reader who has come thus far will understand that I, having come thus far, in twenty-odd years since those days of teetering on the pea-green settee, had always kept Sybaris in the background of my head, as a problem to be solved, and an inquiry to be followed to its completion. There could hardly have been a man in the world better satisfied than I to be the hero of the adventure which I am now about to describe.

If the reader remembers anything about Garibaldi's triumphal entry into Porto Cavallo in Sicily in the spring of 1859, he will remember that, between the months of March and April in that year, the great chieftain made, in that wretched little fishing haven, a long pause, which was not at the time understood by the journals or by their military critics, and which, indeed, to this hour has never been publicly explained. I suppose I know as much about it as any man now living. But I am not writing Garibaldi's memoirs, nor indeed, my own, excepting so far as they relate to Sybaris; and it is strictly nobody's business to inquire as to that detention, unless it interest the ex-king of Naples, who may write to me, if he chooses, addressing Frederic Ingham, Esq., Waterville, N. H. Nor is it anybody's business how long I had then been on Garibaldi's staff. From the number of his staff-officers who have since visited me in America, very much in want of a pair of pantaloons, or a ticket to New York, or something with which they might buy a glass of whiskey, I should think that his staff alone must have made up a much more considerable army than Naples, or even Sybaris, ever brought into the field. But where these men were when I was with him, I do not know. I only know that there was but a handful of us then, hard-worked fellows, good-natured, and not above our duty. Of its military details we knew wretchedly little. But as we had no artillery, ignorance was less dangerous in the chief of artillery; as we had no maps to draw, poor draftsmanship did not much embarrass the engineer in chief. For me, I was nothing but an aid, and I was glad to do anything that fell to me as well as I knew how. And, as usual in human life, I found that a cool head, a steady resolve, a concentrated purpose, and an unselfish readiness to obey, carried me a great way. I listened instead of talking, and thus got a reputation for knowing a great deal. When the time to act came, I acted without waiting for the wave to recede; and thus I sprang into many a boat dry-shod, while people who believed in what is popularly called prudence missed their chance, and either lost the boat or fell into the water.

This is by the way. It was under these circumstances that I received my orders, wholly secret and unexpected, to take a boat at once, pass the straits, and cross the Bay of Tarentum, to communicate at Gallipoli with — no matter whom. Perhaps I was going to the "Castle of Otranto." A hundred years hence anybody who chooses will know. Meanwhile, if there should be a reaction in Otranto, I do not choose to shorten anybody's neck for him.

Well, it was five in the afternoon, — near sundown at that season. I went to dear old Frank Chaney, — the jolliest of jolly Englishmen, who was acting quartermaster-general, — and told him I must have transportation. I can see him and hear him now, — as he sat on his barrel-head, smoked his vile Tunisian tobacco in his beloved short meerschaum, which was left to him ever since he was at Bonn, as he pretended, a student with Prince Albert. He did not swear, — I don't think he ever did. But he looked perplexed enough to swear. And very droll was the twinkle of his eye.

The truth was, that every sort of a thing that would sail, and every wretch of a fisherman that could sail her, had been, as he knew, and as I knew, sent off that very morning to rendezvous at Carrara, for the contingent which we were hoping had slipped through Cavour's pretended neutrality. And here was an order for him to furnish me "transportation" in exactly the opposite direction.

"Do you know of anything, yourself, Fred?" said he.

"Not a coffin," said I.

"Did the chief suggest anything?"

"Not a nutshell," said I.

"Could not you go by telegraph?" said Frank, pointing up to the dumb old semaphore in whose tower he had established himself. "Or has not the chief got a wishing carpet? Or can't you ride to Gallipoli? Here are some excellent white-tailed mules, good enough for Pindar, whom Colvocoressis has just brought in from the monastery. 'Transportation for one!' Is there anything to be brought back? Nitre, powder, lead, junk, hard-tack, mules, horses, pigs, *polenta*, or *olla podrida*, or other of the stores of war?"

No; there was nothing to bring back except myself. Lucky enough if I came back to tell my own story. And so we walked up on the tower deck to take a look.

Blessed St. Lazarus, chief of Naples and of beggars! a little felucca was just rounding the Horse Head and coming into the bay, wing-wing. The fishermen in her had no thought that they were ever going to get into the Atlantic. Maybe they had never heard of the Ocean or of the Monthly. Can that be possible? Frank nodded, and I. He filled up with more Tunisian, beckoned to an orderly, and we walked down to the landing-jetty to meet them.

"*Viva Italia!*" shouted Frank, as they drew near enough to hear.

"*Viva Garibaldi!*" cried the skipper, as he let his sheet fly and rounded to the well-worn stones. A good voyage had they made of it, he and his two brown, ragged boys. Large fish and small, pink fish, blue, yellow, orange, striped fish and mottled, wriggled together, and flapped their tails in the well of the little boat. There were even too many to lie there and wriggle. The bottom of the boat was well covered with them, and, if she had not shipped waves enough to keep them cool, the boy Battista had bailed a plenty on them. Father and son hurried on shore, and Battista on board began to fling the scaly fellows out to them.

A very small craft it was to double all those capes in, run the straits, and stretch across the bay. If it had been mine "to make reply," I should undoubtedly have made this, that I would see the quartermaster hanged, and his superiors, before I risked myself in any such rattletrap. But as, unfortunately, it was mine to go where I was sent, I merely set the orderly to throwing out fish with the boys, and began to talk with the father.

Queer enough, just at that moment, there came over me the feeling that, as a graduate of the University, it was my duty to put up those red, white, and blue scaly fellows, who were flopping about there so briskly, and send them in alcohol to Agassiz. But there are so many duties of that kind which one neglects in a hard-worked world! As a graduate, it is my duty to send annually to the College Librarian a list of all the graduates who have died in the town I live in, with their fathers' and mothers' names, and the motives that led them to College, with anecdotes of their career, and the date of their death. There are two thousand three hundred and forty-five of them I believe, and I have never sent one-half anecdote about one! Such failure in duty made me grimly smile as I omitted to stop and put up these fish in alcohol, and as I plied the unconscious skipper with inquiries about his boat. "Had she ever been outside?" "O signor, she had been outside this very day. You cannot catch *tonno* till you have passed both capes, — least of all such fine fish as that is," — and he kicked the poor wretch. Can it be true, as C—— says, that those dying flaps of theirs are exquisite luxury to them, because for the first time they have their fill of oxygen? "Had he ever been beyond Peloro?" "O yes, signor; my wife, Catarina, was herself from Messina," — and on great saints' days they had gone there often. Poor fellow, his great saint's day sealed his fate. I nodded to Frank, — Frank nodded to me, — and Frank blandly informed him that, by order of General Garibaldi, he would take the gentleman at once on board, pass the strait with him, "and then go where he tells you."

The Southern Italian has the reputation, derived

from Tom Moore, of being a coward. When I used to speak at school,

> "Ay, down to the dust with them, — slaves as they are!" —

stamping my foot at "dust," I certainly thought they were a very mean crew. But I dare say that Neapolitan school-boys have some similar school piece about the risings of Tom Moore's countrymen, which certainly have not been much more successful than the poor little Neapolitan revolution which he was pleased to satirize. Somehow or other, Victor Emanuel is, at this hour, king of Naples. Coward or not, this fine fellow of a fisherman did not flinch. It is my private opinion that he was not nearly as much afraid of the enterprise as I was. I made this observation at the moment with some satisfaction, sent Frank's man up to my lodgings with a note ordering my own traps sent down, and in an hour we were stretching out, under the twilight, across the little bay.

No! I spare you the voyage. Sybaris is what we are after, all this time, if we can only get there. Very easy it would be for me to give you cheap scholarship from the Æneid, about Palinurus and Scylla and Charybdis. Neither Scylla nor Charybdis bothered me, — as we passed wing-wing between them before a smart north wind. I had a little Hunter's Virgil with me, and read the whole voyage, — and confused Battista utterly by trying to make him remember something about Palinuro, of whom he had never heard.

It was much as I afterwards asked my negro waiter at Fort Monroe about General Washington at Yorktown. "Never heard of him, sir, — was he in the Regular army?" So Battista thought Palinuro must have fished in the Italian fleet, with which the Sicilian boatmen were not well acquainted. Messina made no objections to us. Perhaps, if the sloop of war which lay there had known who was lying in the boat under her guns, I might not be writing these words to-day. Battista went ashore, got lemons, macaroni, hard bread, polenta, for themselves, the *Giornale di Messina* for me, and more Tunisian; and, not to lose that splendid breeze, we cracked on all day, passed Reggio, hugged the shore bravely, though it was rough, ran close under those cliffs which are the very end of the Apennines, — will it shock the modest reader if I say the very toe-nails of the Italian foot? — hauled more and more eastward, made Spartivento blue in the distance, made it purple, made it brown, made it green, still running admirably, — ten knots an hour we must have got between four and five that afternoon, — and, by the time the lighthouse at Spartivento was well ablaze, we were abreast of it, and might begin to haul more northward, so that, though we had a long course before us, we should at last be sailing almost directly towards our voyage's end, Gallipoli.

At that moment — as in any sea often happens, if you come out from the more land-locked channel into the larger body of water — the wind appeared to change. Really, I suppose, we came into the steady southwest wind which had probably been drawing all day up toward the Adriatic. In two hours more we made the lighthouse of Stilo, and I was then tired enough to crawl down into the fearfully smelling little cuddy, and, wrapping Battista's heavy storm-jacket round my feet, I caught some sort of sleep.

But not for very long. I struck my watch at three in the morning. And the air was so unworthy of that name, — it was such a thick paste, seeming to me more like a mixture of tar and oil and fresh fish and decayed fish and bilge-water than air itself, — that I voted three morning, and crawled up into the clear starlight, — how wonderful it was, and the fresh wet breeze that washed my face so cheerily! — and I bade Battista take his turn below, while I would lie there and mind the helm. If — if he had done what I proposed, I suppose I should not be writing these lines; but his father, good fellow, said: "No, signor, not yet. We leave the shore now for the broad bay, you see; and if the wind haul southward, we may need to go on the other tack. We will all stay here, till we see what the deep-sea wind may be." So we lay there, humming, singing, and telling stories, still this rampant southwest wind behind, as if all the powers of the Mediterranean meant to favor my mission to Gallipoli. The boat was now running straight before it. We stretched out bravely into the gulf; but, before the wind, it was astonishing how easily the lugger ran. He said to me at last, however, that on that course we were running to leeward of our object; but that it was the best point for his boat, and if the wind held, he would keep on so an hour longer, and trust to the land breeze in the morning to run down the opposite shore of the bay.

"If" again. The wind did not keep on. Either the pole-star, and the dipper, and all the rest of them, had rebelled and were drifting westward, — and so it seemed; or this steady southwest gale was giving out; or, as I said before, we had come into the sweep of a current even stronger, pouring from the Levantine shores of the Mediterranean full up the Gulf of Tarentum. Not ten minutes after the skipper spoke, it was clear enough to both of us that the boat must go about, whether we wanted to or not, and we waked the other boy, to send him forward, before we accepted the necessity. Half asleep, he got up, courteously declined my effort to help him by me as he crossed the boat, stepped round on the gunwale behind me as I sat, and then, either in a lurch or in some misstep, caught his foot in the tiller as his father held it firm, and pitched down directly behind Battista himself, and, as I thought, into the sea. I sprang to leeward to throw something after him, and found him in the sea indeed, but hanging by both hands to the gunwale, safe enough, and in a minute, with Battista's help and mine, on board again. I remember how pleased I was that his father did not swear at him, but only laughed

prettily, and bade him be quick, and step forward; and then turning to the helm, which he had left free for the moment, he did not swear indeed, but he did cry "Santa Madre!" when he found there was no tiller there. The boy's foot had fairly wrenched it, not only from his father's hand, but from the rudder-head, — and it was gone!

We held the old fellow firmly by his feet and legs, as he lay over the stern of the boat, head down, examining the condition of the rudder-head. The report was not favorable. I renewed the investigation myself in the same uncomfortable attitude. The phosphorescence of the sea was but an unsteady light, but light enough there was to reveal what daylight made hardly more certain, — that the wrench which had been given to the rotten old fixtures, shaky enough at best, had split the head of the rudder, so that the pintle hung but loosely in its bed, and that there was nothing available for us to rig a jury tiller on. This discovery, as it became more and more clear to each of us four in succession, abated successively the volleys of advice which we were offering, and sent us back to our more quiet "Santa Madres" or to meditations on "what was next to best."

Meanwhile the boat was flying, under the sail she had before, straight before the wind, up the Gulf of Tarentum.

If you cannot have what you like, it is best, in a finite world, to like what you have. And while the old man brought up from the cuddy his wretched and worthless stock of staves, rope-ends, and bits of iron, and contemplated them ruefully, as if asking them which would like to assume the shape of a rudder-head and tiller, if his fairy godmother would appear on the top of the mast for a moment, I was plying the boys with questions, — what would happen to us if we held on at this tearing rate, and rushed up the bay to the head thereof. The boys knew no more than they knew of Palinuro. Far enough, indeed, were we from their parish. The old man at last laid down the bit of brass which he had saved from some old waif, and listened to me as I pointed out to them on my map the course we were making, and, without answering me a word, fell on his knees and broke into most voluble prayer, — only interrupted by sobs of undisguised agony. The boys were almost as much surprised as I was. And as he prayed and sobbed, the boat rushed on!

Santa Madre, San Giovanni, and Sant' Antonio, — we needed all their help, if it were only to keep him quiet; and when at last he rose from his knees, and came to himself enough to tend the sheets a little, I asked, as modestly as I could, what put this keen edge on his grief or his devotions. Then came such stories of hobgoblins, witches, devils, giants, elves, and fairies, at this head of the bay! — no man ever returned who landed there; his father and his father's father had charged him, and his brothers and his cousins, never to be lured to make a voyage there, and never to run for those coves, though schools of golden fish should lead the way. It was not till this moment, that, trying to make him look upon the map, I read myself there the words, at the mouth of the Crathis River, "Sybari Ruine."

Surely enough, this howling Euroclydon — for Euroclydon it now was — was bearing me and mine directly to Sybaris!

And here was this devout old fisherman confirming the words of Smith's Dictionary, when it said that nobody had been there and returned, for generation upon generation.

At a dozen knots an hour, as things were, I was going to Sybaris! Nor was I many hours from it. For at that moment we cannot have been more than five-and-thirty miles from the beach, where, in less than five hours, Euroclydon flung us on shore.

The memory of the old green settees, and of Hutchinson and Wheeler and the other Latin-school boys, sustained me beneath the calamity which impended. Nor do I think at heart the boys felt so bad as their father about the djins and the devils, the powers of the earth and the powers of the air. Is there, perhaps, in the youthful mind, rather a passion for "seeing the folly" of life a little in that direction? None the less did we join him in rigging out the longest sweep we had aft, lashing it tight under the little rail which we had been leaning on, and trying gentle experiments, how far this extemporized rudder might bring the boat round to the wind. Nonsense the whole! By that time Euroclydon was on us, so that I would never have tried to put her about if we had had the best gear I ever handled, and our experiments only succeeded far enough to show that we were as utterly powerless as men could be. Meanwhile day was just beginning to break. I soothed the old man with such devout expressions as heretic might venture. I tried to turn him from the coming evil to the present necessity. I counselled with him whether it might not be safer to take in sail and drift along. But from this he dissented. Time enough to take in sail when we knew what shore we were coming to. He had no kedge or grapple or cord, indeed, that would pretend to hold this boat against this gale. We would beach her, if it pleased the Virgin; and if we could not, — shaking his head, — why, that would please the Virgin, too.

And so Euroclydon hurried us on to Sybaris.

The sun rose, O how magnificently! Is there anywhere to see sunrise like the Mediterranean? And if one may not be on the top of Katahdin, is there any place for sunrise like the very level of the sea? Already the Calabrian mountains of our western horizon were gray against the sky. One or another of us was forward all the time, trying to make out by what slopes the hills descended to the sea. Was it cliff of basalt, or was it reedy swamp, that was to receive us?

I insisted at last on his reducing sail. For I felt sure that he was driving on under a sort of fatality which made him dare the worst. I was wholly right, for the boat now rose easier on the water, and was much more dry.

Perhaps the wind flagged a little as the sun rose. At all events, he took courage, which I had never lost. I made his boy find us some oranges. I made them laugh by eating their cold polenta with them. I even made him confess, when I called him aft and sent Battista forward, that the shore we were nearing looked low. For we were near enough now to see stone-pines and chestnut-trees. Did anybody see the towers of Sybaris?

Not a tower! But, on the other hand, not a gnome, witch, Norna's Head, or other intimation of the under-world. The shore looked like many other Italian shores. It looked not very unlike what we Yankees call salt-marsh. At all events, we should not break our heads against a wall! Nor will I draw out the story of our anxieties, varying as the waves did on which we rose and fell so easily. As she forged on, it was clear at last that to some wanderers, at least, Sybaris had some hospitality. A long, low spit made out into the sea, with never a house on it, but brown with storm-worn shrubs, above the line of which were the stone-pines and chestnuts which had first given character to the shore. Hard for us, if we had been flung on the outside of this spit. But we were not. Else I had not been writing here to-day. We passed it by fifty fathom clear. Of course under its lee was our harbor. Battista let go the halyards in a moment, and the wet sails came rattling down. The old man, the boy, Battista, and I seized the best sweeps he had left. Two of us at each, working on the same side, we brought her head round as fast as she would bear it in that fearful sea. Inch by inch we wrought along to the smoother water, and breathed free at last as we came under the partial protection of the friendly shore.

Battista and his brother then hauled up the sail enough to give such headway to the boat as we thought our sweeps would control. And we crept along the shore for an hour, seeing nothing but reeds, and now and then a distant buffalo, when at last a very hard knock on a rock the boy ahead had not seen under water started the planks so that we knew that was dangerous play; and, without more solicitation, the old man beached the boat in a little cove where the reeds gave place for a trickling stream. I told them they might land or not, as they pleased. I would go ashore and get assistance or information. The old man clearly thought I was going to ask my assistance from the father of lies himself. But he was resigned to my will, — said he would wait for my return. I stripped and waded ashore with my clothes upon my head, dressed as quickly as I could, and pushed up from the beach to the low upland.

Clearly enough I was in a civilized country. Not that there was a gallows, as the old joke says; but there were tracks in the shingle of the beach showing where wheels had been, and these led me to a cart-track between high growths of that Mediterranean reed which grows all along in those low flats. There is one of the reeds on the hooks above my gun in the hall as you came in. I followed up the track, but without seeing barn, house, horse, or man, for a quarter of a mile, perhaps, when behold, —

Not the footprint of a man! as to Robinson Crusoe; —

Not a gallows and man hanging! as in the sailor story above named; —

But a railroad track! Evidently a horse-railroad.

"A horse-railroad in Italy!" said I, aloud. "A horse-railroad in Sybaris! It must have changed since the days of the coppersmiths!" And I flung myself on a heap of reeds which lay there, and waited.

In two minutes I heard the fast step of horses, as I supposed; in a minute more four mules rounded the corner, and a "horse-car" came dashing along the road. I stepped forward and waved my hand, but the driver bowed respectfully, pointed back, and then to a board on top of his car, and I read, as he dashed by me, the word

Πλήρες,

displayed full above him; as one may read *Complet* on a Paris omnibus.

Now *Πλήρες* is the Greek for full. "In Sybaris they do not let the horse-railroads grind the faces of the passengers," said I. "Not so wholly changed since the coppersmiths." And, within the minute, more quadrupedantal noises, more mules, and another car, which stopped at my signal. I entered, and found a dozen or more passengers, sitting back to back on a seat which ran up the middle of the car, as you might ride in an Irish jaunting-car. In this way it was impossible for the conductor to smuggle in a standing passenger, impossible for a passenger to catch cold from a cracked window, and possible for a passenger to see the scenery from the window. "Can it be possible," said I, "that the traditions of Sybaris really linger here?"

I sat quite in the front of the car, so that I could see the fate of my first friend *Πλήρες*, — the full car. In a very few minutes it switched off from our track, leaving us still to pick up our complement, and then I saw that it dropped its mules, and was attached, on a side track, to an endless chain, which took it along at a much greater rapidity, so that it was soon out of sight. I addressed my next neighbor on the subject, in Greek which would have made my fortune in those old days of the pea-green settees. But he did not seem to make much of that, but in sufficiently good Italian told me, that as soon as we were full, we should be attached in the same way to the chain, which was driven by stationary engines five or six stadia apart, and so indeed it proved. We picked up one or two market-women, a young artist or two, and a little boy. When the child got in, there was a nod and smile on people's faces; my next neighbor said to me, Πλήρες, as if with an air of relief; and sure enough, in a minute more, we were flying along at a 2.20 pace, with neither mule nor engine in sight, stopping about once a mile to drop passengers, if there was need, and evidently approaching Sybaris.

All along now were houses, each with its pretty garden of perhaps an acre, no fences, because no cattle at large. I wonder if the Vineland people know they caught that idea from Sybaris! All the houses were of one story, — stretching out as you remember Pliny's villa did, if Ware and Van Brunt ever showed you the plans, — or as Erastus Bigelow builds factories at Clinton. I learned afterwards that stair-builders and slaveholders are forbidden to live in Sybaris by the same article in the fundamental law. This accounts, with other things, for the vigorous health of their women. I supposed that this was a mere suburban habit, and, though the houses came nearer and nearer, yet as no two houses touched in a block, I did not know we had come into the city till all the passengers left the car, and the conductor courteously told me we were at our journey's end.

When this happens to you in Boston, and you leave your car, you find yourself huddled on a steep, sloping sidewalk, under the rain or snow, with a hundred or more other passengers, all eager, all wondering, all unprovided for. But I found in Sybaris a large glass-roofed station, from which the other lines of neighborhood cars radiated, in which women and even little children were passing from route to route, under the guidance of civil and intelligent persons, who, strange enough, made it their business to conduct these people to and fro, and did not consider it their duty to insult the traveller. For a moment my mind reverted to the contrast at home ; but not long. As I stood admiring and amused at once, a bright, brisk little fellow stepped up to me, and asked what my purpose was, and which way I would go. He spoke in Greek first, but, seeing I did not catch his meaning, relapsed into very passable Italian, quite as good as mine.

I told him that I was shipwrecked, and had come into town for assistance. He expressed sympathy, but wasted not a moment, led me to his chief at an office on one side, who gave me a card with the address of an officer whose duty it was to see to strangers, and said that he would in turn introduce me to the chief of the boat-builders ; and then said, as if in apology for his promptness,

> *Χρὴ ξεῖνον παρεόντα φιλεῖν, ἐθελοντα δὲ πέμπειν,* —
> "Welcome the coming, speed the parting guest."

He called to me a conductor of the red line, said Ξένος, which we translate guest, but which I found in this case means "dead-head," or "free," bowed, and I saw him no more.

"Strange country have I come to, indeed," said I, as I thought of the passports of Civita Vecchia, of the indifference of Scollay's Buildings, and of the surliness of Springfield. "And this is Sybaris!"

WE sent down a tug to the cove which I indicated on their topographical map, and to the terror of the old fisherman and his sons, to whom I had sent a note, which they could not read, our boat was towed up to the city quay, and was put under repairs. That last thump on the hidden rock was her worst injury, and it was a week before I could get away. It was in this time that I got the information I am now to give, partly from my own observations, partly from what George the Proxenus or his brother Philip told me, — more from what I got from a very pleasing person, the wife of another brother, at whose house I used to visit freely, and whose boys, fine fellows, were very fond of talking about America with me. They spoke English very funnily, and like little school-books. The ship-carpenter, a man named Alexander, was a very intelligent person; and, indeed, the whole social arrangement of the place was so simple, that it seemed to me that I got on very fast, and knew a great deal of them in a very short time.

At this point I will, for greater convenience, quote directly from my journal. It has the fault which all journals have, that their memoranda are apt to be fullest when one has the most time to write, and that they are therefore most barren just at those points of crisis when the writer really has most to tell. This remark will be found near the beginning of "John Adams's Journal," of which it is signally true. I will, however, copy what there is in mine. When I find that it fails, I will do my best to supply the deficiency.

JOURNAL.

The πρόξενος, Proxenus, as this officer is called, (officer whose business is to care for strangers, quite after the old Athenian system,) was very civil, though a short-metre kind of person, used evidently to affairs in the time of affairs, and to nothing else. He offered Greek at first for talk, as the man had done at the station; but, finding I preferred Italian, fell into that readily. I am too tired to-night, not to say sleepy, to try to write out much of what he told me, or I told him. He was very expeditious, when he heard about the boat, in sending to her relief. He led me to a good map of the city and harbor which hung on the office wall, and in five minutes had sent a despatch which he said would fit out a tug which would bring the old man and the boys up to the city. I offered to go with them. But he said no, — that I should be of no use there, — or rather of none which a note from me would not serve as well; and that, as I must have had a fatiguing night, I should be much better off at my inn. I observed he used the telegraph constantly, even sending his own despatches by his own instrument, at his office desk, — writing as readily so as I do these words. In answer to a question of mine, he said there were delivery offices almost everywhere, and that they hardly ever had occasion to use a special messenger. But, when he wanted to send my note to the tug, and afterwards to send me here, he beckoned to his son, a tall, pleasant-looking boy, who brought me, to show me the way.*

The inn covers a good deal of ground for the number of rooms, but there is not a staircase in it. It is not larger than a generous private house. The whole is of one story, as is every other house I have so far seen in Sybaris. The mistress is a jolly-looking person, who for all her jollity seems careful and thoughtful, and desirous to be of service; and, without worrying me, she has really made me very comfortable. She knocked just now herself, and, in quite a studied speech, said that I was the first American she had ever had here; that she was wholly unacquainted with our customs, but that she would be much obliged to me if

* After I knew the Proxenus better, I told him that this ready and constant use of the telegraph was one of the first of their conveniences I noticed. He said the telegraph was an old affair with them, and he wondered other nations had been so slow in copying it; that they used it as long ago as what he called their day of horrors, when Sybaris was crushed by the Crotoniates, more than five centuries before Christ. I was amazed at this, but in their public library afterwards I found in Pliny that that defeat was known at Olympia in Greece on the day it happened, and the same statement is in Cicero *De Naturâ Deorum*. See Pliny, VII. 22. (1), and compare Plutarch in *Paulus Æmilius*, where he names four such incidents.

I would indicate to her any improvements which the inns of my own country might suggest to me. The poor soul had been at the pains to look up "United States" in some book of travels, and had even written to the Proxenus to ask how she should cook pork and beans for me, and what she should give me instead of salt codfish. He had written her a funny note, which she showed me, in which he said that I should be satisfied with pheasants and quails for a day, and that the next day he would tell her.

Experience of my own country indeed! There was not a fly in the room where the *table d'hôte* is served, nor is there in this apartment. This consists of a pretty, airy sitting-room with a veranda opening from it, and in the next room the bed and its appurtenances. I found on the table pen, ink, and paper, which I never found ready in my own room at the Brevoort; I found in the bedroom a foot-tub, a shower-bath, more towels than I could count, and hot and cold water ready to run for me. I have not smelled a smell since I came into the house, excepting the savory breakfast and dinner which she gave me, and these lovely Italian violets which stand on the writing-table; and, of course, my cigar on the veranda. But I shall write no more. Now we will see if there are any smooth rose-leaves in the beds of Sybaris.

That is the end of that day's entry.

The Proxenus came round to see me that first evening, and we sat, smoking, on the piazza together. I remember I spoke with pleasure of the horse-railroad management, and asked as to the methods they took to secure such personal comfort.

He said that my question cut pretty low down, for that the answer really involved the study of their whole system. "I have thought of it a good deal," said he, "when I have been in St. Petersburg, and in England and America; and as far as I can find out, our peculiarity in everything is, that we respect — I have sometimes thought we almost worshipped — the rights, even the notions or whims, of the individual citizen. With us the first object of the state, as an organization, is to care for the individual citizen, be he man, woman, or child. We consider the state to be made for the better and higher training of men, much as your divines say that the Church is. Instead of our lumping our citizens, therefore, and treating Jenny Lind and Tom Heenan to the same dose of public schooling, — instead of saying that what is sauce for the goose is sauce for the gander, — we try to see that each individual is protected in the enjoyment, not of what the majority likes, but of what he chooses, so long as his choice injures no other man."

I thought, in one whiff, of Stuart Mill, and of the coppersmiths.

"Our horse-railroad system grew out of this theory," continued he. "As long ago as Herodotus, people lived here in houses one story high, with these gardens between. But some generations ago, a young fellow named Apollidorus, who had been to Edinburgh, pulled down his father's house and built a block of what you call houses on the site of it. They were five stories high, had basements, and so on, with windows fore and aft, and, of course, none on the sides. The old fogies looked aghast. But he found plenty of fools to hire them. But the tenants had not been in a week when the Kategoros, district attorney, had him up 'for taking away from a citizen what he could not restore.' This, you must know, is one of the severest charges in our criminal code.

"Of course, it was easy enough to show that the tenants went willingly; he showed dumb-waiters, and I know not what infernal contrivances of convenience within. But he could not show that the tenants had north windows and south windows, because they did not. The government, on their side, showed that men were made to breathe fresh air, and that he could not ventilate his houses as if they were open on all sides; they showed that women were not made to climb up and down ladders, and to live on stages at the tops of them; and he tried in vain to persuade the jury that this climbing was good for little children. He had lured these citizens into places dangerous for health, growth, strength, and comfort. And so he was compelled to erect a statue typical of strength, and a small hospital for infants, as his penalty. That spirited Hercules, which stands in front of the market, was a part of his fine.

" Of course, after a decision like this, concentration of inhabitants was out of the question. Every pulpit in Sybaris blazed with sermons on the text, ' Every man shall sit under his vine and under his fig-tree.' Everybody saw that a house without its own garden was an abomination, and easy communication with the suburbs was a necessity.

" It was, indeed, easy enough to show, as the city engineer did, that the power wasted in lifting people up, and, for that matter, down stairs, in a five-story house, in one day, would carry all those people I do not know how many miles on a level railroad track in less time. What you call horse-railroads, therefore, became a necessity."

I said they made a great row with us.

" Yes," said he, " I saw they did. With us the government owns and repairs the track, as you do the track of any common road. We never have any difficulty.

" You see," he added after a pause, " with us, if a conductor sprains the ankle of a citizen, it is a matter the state looks after. With you, the citizen must himself be the prosecutor, and virtually never is. Did you notice a pretty winged Mercury outside the station-house you came to ? "

I had noticed it.

" That was put up, I don't know how long ago, in the infancy of these things. They took a car off one night, without public notice beforehand. One old man was coming in on it, to his daughter's wedding.

He missed his connection out at Little Krastis, and lost half an hour. Down came the Kategoros. The company had taken from a citizen what they could not restore, namely, half an hour."

George lighted another cigar, and laughed very heartily. "That 's a great case in our reports," he said. "The company ventured to go to trial on it. They hoped they might overturn the old decisions, which were so old that nobody knows when they were made, — as old as the dancing horses," said he, laughing. "They said *time* was not a thing, — it was a relation of ideas; that it did not exist in heaven; that they could not be made to suffer because they did not deliver back what no man ever saw, or touched, or tasted. What was half an hour? But the jury was pitiless. A lot of business men, you know, — they knew the value of time. What did they care for the metaphysics? And the company was bidden to put up an appropriate statue worth ten talents in front of their station-house, as a reminder to all their people that a citizen's time was worth something."

I observed a queer thing two or three times in this visit of the Proxenus. Just at this point he rose rather suddenly and bade me good evening. I begged him to stay, but had to repeat my invitation twice. His hand was on the handle of the door before he turned back. Then he sat down, and we went on talking; but before long he did the same thing again, and then again.

At last I was provoked, and said: "What is the custom of your country? Do you have to take a walk every eleven minutes and a quarter?"

George laughed again, and indeed blushed. "Do you know what a bore is?" said he.

"Alas! I do," said I.

"Well," said he, "the universal custom here is, that an uninvited guest, who calls on another man on his own business, rises at the end of eleven minutes, and offers to go. And the courts have ruled, very firmly, that there must be a *bona fide* effort. We get into such a habit of it, that, with you, I really did it unawares. The custom is as old as Cleisthenes and his wedding. But some of the decisions are not more than two or three centuries old, and they are very funny.

"On the whole," he added, "I think it works well. Of course, between friends, it is absurd, but it is a great protection against a class of people who think their own concerns are the only things of value. You see you have only to say, when a man comes in, that you thank him for coming, that you wish he would stay, or to take his hat or his stick, — you have only to make him an invited guest, — and then the rule does not hold."

"Ah!" said I; "then I invite you to spend every evening with me while I am here."

"Take care," said he; "the Government Almanac is printed and distributed gratuitously from the fines on bores. Their funds are getting very low up at the department, and they will be very sharp on your friends. So you need not be profuse in your invitations.

THIS conversation was a clew to a good many things which I saw while I was in the city. I never was in a place where there were so many tasteful, pretty little conveniences for everybody. At the quadrants, where the streets cross, there was always a pretty little sheltered seat for four or five people, — shaded, stuffed, dry, and always the morning and evening papers, and an advertisement of the times of boats and trains, for any one who might be waiting for a car or for a friend. Sometimes these were votive offerings, where public spirit had spoken in gratitude. More often they had been ordered at the cost of some one who had taken from a citizen what he could not repay. The private citizen might often hesitate about prosecuting a bore, or a nuisance, or a conceited company officer. But the Kategoroi made no bones about it. They called the citizen as a witness, and gave the criminal a reminder which posterity held in awe. Their point, as they always explained it to me, is, that the citizen's health and strength are essential to the state. The state cannot afford to have him maimed, any more than it can afford to have him drunk or ignorant. The individual, of course, cannot be following up his separate grievances with people who abridge his rights. But the public accuser can and does.

With us, public servants, who know they are public servants, are always obliging and civil. I would not ask better treatment in my own home than I am sure of in Capitol, State-house, or city hall. It is only when you get to some miserable sub-bureau, where the servant of the servant of a creature of the state can bully you, that you come to grief. For instance, the State of Massachusetts just now forbids corporations to work children more than ten hours a day. The *corporations* obey. But the overseers in the rooms, whom the corporations employ, work children eleven hours, or as many as they choose. They would not stand that in Sybaris.

Such were my first day's observations. I now resume the Journal of which I have spoken.

Friday, 9th Kal. Θαργηλιών. — Everything seems to be new here. Place, language, and all are changed, — and so my old book for these memoranda gave out last night, and I have had to rummage up another from my stores. Fortunately the traps came up from the boat even before I was awake this morning. One does sleep well in such a bed, — without steam-whistles or cockerels or brass-founders. It was as quiet as the mid-country.

The calendar is as new as the book (of which the paper is not half as good as the old was). It seems an odd mixture of Italian and Greek, and I do not yet understand it. But I put at the top of the page what the Proxenus tells me to, were it only for practice. This is, he says, the ninth of the Kalends of Thargelion, but he counts it Friday, as I did. For my part, I thought the Greeks had no Kalends; but it would seem that the Sybarites have.

It has been a rainy day, but I have managed with their convenient arrangements here to do about ten times as much as I should have done at home. If I do not get too sleepy, I will go into a little more detail than I have been apt to do since the campaign began. The peculiarity of this place seems to be, that everybody has plenty of time.

I slept late after the excitement of the night before, and if the lady Myrtis's nice mattresses are made of rose-leaves, none of the leaves were crumpled. I rang, as I had been bidden, as soon as I woke; and a ravishing cup of coffee appeared almost on the moment, on the strength of which I dressed slowly, and went down to the *table d'hôte.* Breakfast was very nicely served; but I do not stop to describe it, because some rainy day I will make a chapter on the cookery of Sybaris, so different from that of our Sicilian allies; alas! so different from the taverns of my beloved New England. While I was at breakfast there came in this clever little note in this pretty Greek *Handschrift* from the Proxenus, whose name, it appears, is George:—

[Translation.]

OFFICE OF THE PROXENUS,
Sybaris, 9th Kal. Thar.

COLONEL INGHAM, &c., &c.: —

DEAR SIR, — The report from Pylades, chief of boat-builders, is that your boat will require a new stern-post as well as rudder, and that one whole streak on her larboard side must be renewed. She was ordered to the government works last night, and the men undoubtedly went to work on her this morning.

I shall have the pleasure of calling on you at seven minutes after noon, when I shall be relieved from office duty here. If you have no pleasanter engagement, let me take you in my carriage to see our granite quarries and to bathe. We can do this before dinner. My wife will be very happy if you will join our family party at four.

Farewell,
GEORGE, *the Proxenus.*

What his other name is, I do not yet know. They seem to sign like English bishops.

I strayed round a little before noon, and made a little sketch of a seat for passengers waiting for the street railroad cars. At twelve I rendered myself on the hotel veranda, and at seven minutes past the Proxenus drove up in a pretty covered buggy, with a nice little trotting mare. He apologized for the cover;

said, if the day had been fine he could have shown me more of the country, but as it rained, why, we must e'en bear it as we could.

We drove first to the granite quarries, which are worked with great precision by a fine-looking set of men, who have much more of the Lombard, not to say Yankee, look about them in their promptness of movement than I have seen anywhere else in Southern Italy. Then the Proxenus asked me if I were used to swimming as early as this in the season. When I said there were few seasons and few waters in which I did not swim, and that I should greatly enjoy a plunge, he turned his horse's head, and we drove, by a charming up-and-down-hill drive, I should think six miles, down the old course of the Crastis River till we came to a signal-station, — what one might call Watch Hill, — where was a beautiful view of the gulf, grand bluffs, smooth beaches, and a fine surf for bathers. It almost seemed as if we had been expected. A quaint old fisherman fastened the horse to a fence, provided towels, pointed out two little sheds for undressing, and we had a brisk swim in the surf. How delicious this Mediterranean water is, swept off the Syrtes by that tremendous Euroclydon! I hardly thought yesterday morning that I should be speaking of it so good-naturedly.

Home to dinner. The Proxenus said his wife would excuse my frock-coat. And at his house, at dinner, and in the garden, and on the veranda, I have stayed ever since, till now. The family was charming, — his wife sweet pretty (reminds you of S—— G——), and seven children, — four boys, three girls, — my friend James, who showed me the way yesterday, being the second son. He and I are great friends, and his father says I may take him from the office any day when I want a guide. The girls have pretty Greek faces, — the youngest about as big as little Fan-fan, only her name is Anna, say nine years old.

As for the dinner, I leave that till I can write the essay on cookery into which the breakfast is to go. But I do not wonder that that old fellow took his cooks with him when he went from here to Athens.

It was not exactly the family party which the note promised. The Chief Justice was there, — who, if I understand, is the cousin of my hostess, — and his pretty wife; a young man named Joannes Isocrates, whom I accused of being a great-grandson of the orator; and Philip, the brother of the Proxenus. It was a round table for twelve. Some of the children had to sit at a side table, and they were very merry there.

The talk was very ready and free, — generally general; but sometimes I got off into a separate private talk with Kleone — as I shall begin to call George's wife — and with the Chief Justice's wife. Her husband calls her Lois. We sat long at table, spending more than half the time over the fruit and coffee. There was no wine. The dessert, however, had been served in another room than that we ate the meats in. We passed from room to room, as we used to when we dined with Howqua, at Canton. And in the new room we did not take the same places as before.

I said, in the course of talk, that either they were all very much at leisure here, or that I had taken an unconscionable amount of George's time. . . . .

He laughed, and said he could well believe that, as I had said that I was brought up in Boston. "When I was there," said he, "I could see that your people were all hospitable enough, but that the people who were good for anything were made to do all the work of the *vauriens*, and really had no time for friendship or hospitality. I remember an historian of yours, who crossed with me, said that there should be a motto stretched across Boston Bay, from one fort to another, with the words, 'No admittance, except on business.'"

I did not more than half like this chaffing at Boston, and asked how they managed things in Sybaris.

"Why, you see," said he, "we hold pretty stiffly to the old Charondian laws, of which perhaps you know something; here 's a copy of the code, if you would like to look over it," and he took one out of his pocket. "We are still very chary about amendments to statutes, so that very little time is spent in legislation; we have no bills at shops, and but little debt, and that is all on honor, so that there is not much account-keeping or litigation; you know what happens to gossips, — gossip takes a good deal of time elsewhere, — and somehow everybody does his share of work, so that all of us do have a good deal of what you call 'leisure.' Whether," he added pensively, "in a world God put us into that we might love each other, and learn to love, — whether the time we spend in society, or the time we spend caged behind our office desks, is the time which should be called devoted to the 'business of life,' that remains to be seen."

"How came you to Boston," said I, "and when?"

"O, we all have to travel," said George, "if we mean to go into the administration. And I liked administration. I observe that you appoint a foreign ambassador because he can make a good stump speech in Kentucky. But, since Charondas's time, training has been at the bottom of our system. And no man could offer himself here to serve on the school committee, unless he knew how other nations managed their schools."

"Not if he had himself made school-books?" said I.

"No!" laughed George, "for he might introduce them. With us no professor may teach from a text-book he has made himself, unless the highest council of education order it; and, on the same principle, we should never choose a bookseller on the school committee. And so, to go back," he said, "when my father found that administration was my passion, he sent me the grand tour. I learned a great deal in

America, and am very fond of the Americans. But I never saw one here before."

I did not ask what he learned in America, for I was more anxious to learn myself how they administered government in Sybaris.

The Chief Justice said that he thought George hardly answered my question. He said that their system compelled everybody to do what he could do best, and to a large extent secured this by inviting people to do what they could do best. A messenger in a public office, for instance, is invariably a man who has legs and a tongue, but who has no arms. That is, if such a place is vacant, search is at once made for some person who shall fill this place well; and if he can show that there is no other place he can fill, on that showing he is almost sure of the appointment. "We have not a copying-clerk in the Court-House," said the Chief Justice, "who has two legs. Most of them, in fact, have no tongues, which is a convenience." Starting from this, as George had said, it followed that there were no *vauriens*, and of course the amount of work fell lighter on each. But this is not the whole. Custom in part, statute in part, and in part this terrible verdict which they all so dread, — the verdict of ἁρπαγμός they call it,* — have so wrought on them

* The verdict of ἁρπαγμός is that alluded to above. It is given on an indictment brought by the state's attorney in a criminal court. It means, "He has taken from a citizen what he cannot restore." The derivation reminds one of our action of *assumpsit*, but they carry it further than we do.

that they destroy very little which they have once created. "Time will do that for us," said Philip, laughing. "My rear wall tumbles down fast enough without my helping the fall."

I said I remembered that Judge Merrick said that, if the thousand million men now in the world could be set to work in intelligent organized labor, they could in a generation duplicate the present monuments of the race of men. The existing farms, roads, bridges, ships, piers, cities, villages, and all the rest, could be produced in one generation. All the other generations have been spent in men's cutting each other's throats, and in destroying what other people have been at work upon.

The Chief Justice said this was undoubtedly true. They tried as far as they could to prevent such waste of life, and to a large extent he thought they succeeded. The solidity of their building is such that they have dwelling-houses which have been occupied as such for two thousand years.

I said that in London they had told me their houses tumbled down in eighty.

"Exactly," said the Chief Justice, "and what a waste that is! When my father was in London, they were greatly delighted with a system of sewers they had just turned into the Thames. When I was there, they were as much delighted, because they had discovered a method of leading their contents away from the Thames."

"When my father was in Boston," said George, "they were all very proud to show him their success in digging down their highest hill. When I was there they were building it up to the old height, to make a reservoir on top of it."

"We have come to the conclusion," said the Chief Justice, "that it is rather dangerous interfering much with nature. That is to say, when a large body of men have nestled down in a region, it was probably about what they wanted. If one of them tries to mend, he is apt to mar. We had a fellow over on the Crastis there, who was stingy about using steam-power; so he made a great high dam on the river, — and, by Jupiter, Colonel Ingham, five hundred thousand people lost their fish because that fellow chose to spin cotton a ten-millionth part of a drachma cheaper than the rest of mankind."

"He got ἁρπαγμός with a vengeance," growled Philip, who is a little touchy.

"He got ἁρπαγμός," said the Chief Justice, "and he had to put in fish-ways. You must take our friend out to see the fish go up his stairways, George. But what happened at Pæstum was worse than that. They had some salt marshes there, — what they call flats. They undertook to fill them up so as to get land in place of water. They got more than they bargained for. They disturbed the natural flow of the currents, and they lost their harbor. Land is plenty in Pæstum now. The last time I was there the population was two owls and four lizards, and there was never a rose within five miles!"

I called him back to talk of this universal occupation, resulting in universal leisure. He said I should understand it better after I had been about a little. I said we had difficulty at both ends, — the poorest people did not know how to work, and the richest people were apt not to want to, and did not know what to do. I said I was at one time secretary of the "Society for providing Occupation for the Higher Classes." He said, as to the first they clung to the old apprenticeship system. Every child must be taught to do something. If the parents cannot teach, somebody else does. The other difficulty he had seen in travelling, but he did not believe it was necessary. They have here but few very large fortunes transmitted from father to son. They have no such transmission by will, and unless a man has given away his property before his death the state becomes his executor. Of course in practice, except in cases of sudden death, people are their own executors. Then they give every man and woman who is over sixty-five a small pension, — enough to save anybody from absolute want. They insist on it that this is the most convenient arrangement. They know almost nothing of drunkenness; and what follows is, that everybody does something somewhere.

As the chief explained this to me, I saw his wife and Philip were laughing about something, and when the learned talk was done Philip made her tell me what it was. It was the story of one of their attempts to save time, which had not succeeded so well. Two or three enterprising fellows, in those arts which rank as the disagreeable necessities, went into partnership, offering to their customers the saving of time gained by getting through the minor miseries together. You sat in a chair to have your hair cut, and a dentist at the same time filled your teeth.* Then you were permitted at the same time to have any man up who wanted to read his poems to you, and you could hear them as you sat. While the dentist was rolling up the gold, they had a photograph man ready to take your likeness. Lois declared she would show me a likeness of her husband that was so savage she was sure it was taken there. But of course this was running the thing into the ground. It was only an exaggeration, and did not last after the novelty was gone.

I said they certainly had got the right men in the right places in administration, as far as I had seen, bowing to the Proxenus.

He parried the compliment by pretending to think I meant the railroad people, and said I was right there, that they had a very good staff in the transportation department.

I said that we had tried the experiment, in some cases, of placing idiots in charge of the minor rail-

* I believe a part of the plan was to have a chiropodist look at your feet; but at table they did not speak of that.

way stations, and to drive the little railway caos or flies from such stations. He said he had observed this in America, but he should not think it would work well. I said the passengers generally knew what they wanted, — that we had an excellent class of men as train conductors, and that these idiots must be put somewhere. Yes, he said, but that you never could tell what station might be important; that I might depend upon it it was cheaper in the long run to have a man competent for the full conceivable duty of the place, even if we had to pay him something more.

About eight o'clock I bowed myself out. George walked home with me, and again we had a cigar on the veranda. They raise their own tobacco, in some cross valleys they have, running east and west, and the cigars are splendid, — real Vuelta d'Abajo, I should have thought them. But of course, under such laws, no man can smoke in the streets or in a crowd.

Saturday, Θαργηλιών, 8*th Kal.* — A fine day. But I find one does not rise very early in the morning.

Spent the morning from nine to twelve with the Chief Justice in court. Business very prompt, very interesting, of which more at another time. I have full notes of all the cases, in the printed briefs which the Judge gave me. At twelve the court closed with absolute promptness. All their public offices of administration work four public hours, as they say. But an office where one calls for information — as the Post-

Office, the Public Library, or any of the charities — is open night and day the century round. The Public Library has not been closed, they say, since Herodotus wrote there. They showed me his pen, and the place where he sat. This seems a little mythical. Of course the same people are not on duty. But they say there is no harm in changing clerks on duty. There can be no secrets then, no false accounts, no peculation, and no ruts. At all events, they say, that if a man chooses to go and read at three in the morning, he has a right to; and that the Post-Office is established for the convenience of the citizen, and not for that of the clerks, which certainly seems true.

The Chief Justice, at twelve, said he was at my service; and at my request he took me to the Public Library, where we spent a couple of hours, — of which at another time. We then called at his house, where we found his wife and daughters just entering their carriage. We did not leave his little wagon, but all drove off together. The object was again a bath, with a chowder and fish dinner at a little extemporized sea-shore place. The drive was charming, and the bath Elysium. The ladies bathed with us. I complimented Mrs. Lois, as I led her down into the surf, on their punctuality, — saying that they had not kept us waiting an instant. But she hardly understood me. "Why should we have kept you?" said she. "I had a despatch at noon from my husband, proposing that we should all start at two." And when I asked if they had been waiting, "Why should we have been waiting?" said she. "We all knew you were not to be at home before two." The Chief Justice laughed and said: "People are so used to punctuality here, that Lois, who is a home-body, hardly knows what you are talking about. The truth is, that, if she had kept you thirty seconds, while she went back for her gloves, she would have been afraid of ἁρπαγμός; and these girls, — why, if one of their watches had been a twenty-thousandth part of a second wrong when the ball fell at noon to-day, I should have had no peace till I had bought such a love of a diamond-mounted little repeater that there is at Archippus's." And he laughed at his joke heartily, and the girls said, "O papa!"

Girls and boys, men and women, all swim like fishes, — taught at a very early age. No scholar is permitted to go forward in any school after seven years of age, unless he can swim, just as we require vaccination. "If you mean to be at the charge of training them," said the Chief Justice, "it is a pity to have them drowned, just when they are fit for anything." And so we had a brisk, jolly swim, and dressed, and went to old Strepsiades's little cabin, where were fish baked, fish broiled, fish cooked in every which way conceivable, hot from the coals, and we with the real sea appetite. We lounged round on the bluffs and shore for an hour or two, the girls sketched and botanized a little, and by another pretty drive we came home. I took a cup of tea with them, came back here to dress, and they then called for me and took me to a pretty dancing-party. But I am too tired to write it out to-night. *Χαῖρε.*

Sunday, 7th Kal. Tharg. — We have a lovely morning. I have this pretty little note from the charming Kleone, asking me whether I will go to their little parish church or to the more grand cathedral service. Of course I have elected the parish church with them at eleven. Meanwhile, I seize this half-hour to fill out one or two gaps above.

I see I have said nothing about their going and coming. The sidewalks are all well laid; and I have thus far been nowhere where, on one side of the way at least, there was not one in perfect order. But I can see that they are very much tempted not to walk; and I think they get their exercise more in rowing, swimming, riding, drill, and so on. This shows itself in the fine chests of boys and girls, men and women. Not only are the public conveyances admirable, and dog-cheap, — very rapid too, so that you feel as if you could hardly afford to walk, — but they have any number of little steam dog-carts, which run on the public rail, or, if necessary, on the hard Macadam road. The fuel is naphtha, or what we call petroleum; the engines are really high-pressure, but the discharge-pipe opens into a chamber kept very cold by freezing mixtures, which you can change at any inn. Philip who told me about these things, says they are used, not so much as being better than horses, but as an economy for that immense class of people who keep no servants, do not choose to be slaves to a coachman, have no one to care for a horse, or indeed do not want the bother. This little steam-wagon stands in a shed at the back of the house. Whoever fills the other lamps fills and trims the wicks of their burners. When you sit down to breakfast, you light the lamps. And when your breakfast is done, steam is up, and you can drive directly to your store or office. While you are there, it stands a month if you choose, and is a bill of expense to nobody. It gives the roads a very brisk look to see these little things spinning along everywhere.

The party last night was charming in the freshness and variety and ease of the whole thing. I hope the host and hostess enjoyed it as much as I did, and they seemed to. How queer the effect of this individuality is when you come to see it in costume! Of course the whole thing was Greek. You saw that, from the girls' faces down to the buckles of their slippers. But then the individual right, to which everything I have seen in Sybaris seems dedicated, appeared all through, and fairly made the whole seem like a fancy ball. If I thought of Gell's Greek costumes, it was only to think how he would have stared if anybody had told him that a hundred and fifty miles from Naples, would he only risk the cutting of his throat by brigands, he might see the thing illustrated so prettily. I danced with —— Philip has come to take me to church.

Finished the same evening.—It was a pretty little church,—quite open and airy it would seem to us,—excellent chance to see dancing vines, or flying birds, or falling rains, or other "meteors outside," if the preacher proved dull or the hymns undevout. But I found my attention was well held within. Not that the preaching was anything to be repeated. The sermon was short, unpretending, but alive and devout. It was a sonnet, all on one theme; that theme pressed, and pressed, and pressed again, and, of a sudden, the preacher was done. "You say you know God loves you," he said. "I hope you do, but I am going to tell you once more that he loves you, and once more and once more." What pleased me in it all was a certain unity of service, from the beginning to the end. The congregation's singing seemed to suggest the prayer; the prayer seemed to continue in the symphony of the organ; and, while I was in revery, the organ ceased; but as it was ordered, the sermon took up the theme of my revery, and so that one theme ran through the whole. The service was not ten things, like the ten parts of a concert, it was one act of communion or worship. Part of this was due, I guess, to this, that we were in a small church, sitting or kneeling near each other, close enough to get the feeling of communion,—not parted, indeed, in any way. We had been talking together, as we stood in the churchyard before the service began, and when we assembled in the church the sense of sympathy continued. I told Kleone that I liked the home feeling of the church, and she was pleased. She said she was afraid I should have preferred the cathedral. There were four large cathedrals, open, as the churches were, to all the town; and all the clergy, of whatever order, took turns in conducting the service in them. There were seven successive services in each of them that Sunday. But each clergyman had his own special charge beside,— I should think of not more than a hundred families. And these families, generally neighbors in the town indeed, seemed, naturally enough, to grow into very familiar personal relations with each other.

Father Thomas, as they all call him, took me home to his house to dinner. He had one of those little steam-wagons which I have described, of which there were sixty-five standing in the grounds around the church. His wife and children went home in a large one. As soon as the doxology was sung and the benediction pronounced, the sexton went round with a lantern and lighted their lamps, and while we stood round talking in the porch, the steam was got up, so that I suppose everybody was off in twenty minutes. Father Thomas said the talk then and there, in the church and in the porch, was one of the most satisfactory parts of the whole service, and was pleased when I quoted μὴ ἐγκαταλείποντες τὴν ἐπισυναγωγὴν ἑαυτῶν.* I said I had never heard the Greek of the Greek Testament read in service before. He said that the people all followed, with entire interest and understanding of it, though it is not as near their Greek as our Bible is to modern English, and probably never would be. For they regard their Greek as being better than the Attic Greek of Demosthenes's time, — and of course they will not cede an inch towards the Alexandrianisms of late centuries. "Indeed," said he, "the Academy and the Aristarchs are a deal too stiff about it. They are very hard on us theologues, and seem to me absurd."

Father Thomas's house is one such as they say there are a great many of, which show their only concession to a community system. With all this intense individualism, one can see that Robert Owen would hang himself here. But Father Thomas says this arrangement works well, and is a great economy both in time and money. Four houses, each with its half-acre garden, standing near each other, there is built, just on the corner where the lots meet, a central house, — *μεσοικία*, they call it, — for the common purposes of the four. There is one kitchen, and they unite in hiring one cook, who gets up all the meals for the four several families in their own homes, according to their several directions. There is one large playroom for the children. I asked if there were one nurse; but he said, not generally, though families settled that as

* "Not forsaking the assembling of ourselves together."

they chose. What he laid most stress on was one book-room or library for the four. And certainly this was a lovely room. There were four bookcases,— one on each side, — which held severally the books of the four families. All Father Thomas's were together. But, in the long run, it happened that none of them duplicated the other's books, so far as they kept them in this room. There would be but one Herodotus, one Dante, one Shakespeare, one French Dictionary, for the four. Then this room made a pleasant place of reunion among the families, without mutual invitation, and without the feeling that you might be boring the others. Indeed, I spent the evening there, — as will appear, if this narrative ever comes down to the evening.

In the afternoon I had a long walk with Father Thomas in his parish. We went first to one of the four cathedrals, where he had the three o'clock service. The congregation was from all parts of the town and neighborhood, — many people attending there, he said, who never went to any of the parish churches. The different clergymen take these services in order. I should think there were four or five thousand persons here. The service lasted an hour, and he then took me from place to place with him, showing me, as he said, how people lived. And so I have had, in very short time, insight into a wider range of homes than I have ever had in Europe. Everywhere comfort, and the most curious illustrations of what comfort is.

Their system seems to give more definiteness to the work of the clergy and of the churches than ours does. Thus Father Thomas preaches regularly in the church I was in this morning (τῆς Ζωῆς αἰωνίου is its name, — the Church of Life Eternal). There gather perhaps a hundred families, from all parts of the city and neighborhood. And, as I understand it, his relations to them are much like those of one of our Congregational ministers to his flock, — say Haliburton's to his in Cairo, or mine to my people when I was settled in Naguadavick. But this is rather a personal relation between him and these people, who have, so to speak, gravitated towards him. He preaches there usually once every Sunday, and, as I understand it, our practice of exchanging pulpits is wholly unknown. They would be as much surprised, on going into the "Church of Life Eternal," to find any minister but Father Thomas, as they would be, on going into court for the trial of a case, to find that the counsel they had engaged had made an "exchange" with some other man, who had come to plead in his place. As I have said, the service here seems to be regarded, at law at least, as a secondary part of the matter. This Church of Life Eternal is regarded as in a thousand ways responsible for a whole *νομός* or territorial district, in one corner of which, indeed, it stands. It is exactly like the theory of our territorial parish; but they do not use the word "parish," *παροικία*, or rather they use it for a different thing. Everybody in the nomos of "Life Eternal," numbering say four hundred families, is under the oversight, not so much of Father Thomas, as of all the committees, visitors, deacons, deaconesses, and people with names unknown to me, who are the workers of this church. "Under the oversight" means that this church would be disgraced if there were a typhus-fever district in this nomos, or if a family starved to death here, or if there were a drunken row. It would be considered that the church of the nomos was not doing the thing for which churches are established here.

Father Thomas reminded me that, in the newspaper reports of criminal trials, I always see, next the name of the offender, the name of his nomos, as "South Congregational," "St. Paul's," "Old North," "Disciples'," — "Life Eternal," said he, "if we had been so unlucky. But none of our people have been before the court for thirty-one years. In consequence," he said, "if such a misfortune did happen to us, I should not hear the last of it for a month. Every man I met in the street would stop me to sympathize with me; and I should know that people considered that we had made some bad mistake in our arrangements, if we should have a series of such things happen. Of course, we cannot help people's throwing themselves away. But it is supposed that, if Christianity means anything, it means that Jesus Christ came to take away the sins of the world; and this church is regarded as his representative, at least so far as that vulgar or concrete form of sin goes which men call crime."

I take it this arrangement by which a fixed organization is responsible in every locality for the prevention of poverty and the prevention of crime has a great deal to do with the curious insignificance of their criminal business in the courts.

I am terribly tired, but feel as if I understood them a little better than I did yesterday. *Χαῖρε.*

Monday, 6*th*. — A busy day; but, warned by yesterday, I have not fagged myself out as I did then. Or, rather, I ought to say, I have taken their advice, instead of living in my own fashion. I am really becoming a Sybarite myself, and therefore sit down here at 9.30 at night, not dead knocked up by the day's work, as a Yankee would be, and as I was yesterday.

The programme was, breakfast with the boat-builder Pylades; then to go through the schools with Kleone, who takes a good deal of interest in them; to drive and bathe with Philip's people; to dine with the Angelides, — nice people whom I met at the party, Friday, — and with them go to their theatre, where their daughters were to act. All this is over, and I am here at 9.30, as before said.

They make much account of breakfast parties. I noticed on Saturday, that the Chief Justice said he liked to see people before they had begun to go to sleep, and that most people did begin to go to sleep at noon. Here was, at eight o'clock in the morning, a charming party, just evenly divided between men and women, round a large, circular table, in a beautiful room opening on a veranda. The table blazed with flowers, and even with early fruit from the forcing-houses. I took out Kleone, but the talk was general.

I asked Philip how long his brother would remain in the office of Proxenus. Philip turned a little sharply on me, and asked if I had any complaints to make. I soothed him by explaining that all that I asked about was the term of office in their system, and he apologized.

"He will be in as long as he chooses, probably. In theory he remains in until a majority of the voters, which is to say the adult men and women, join in a petition for his removal. Then he will be removed at once. The government will appoint a temporary substitute, and order an election of his successor."

"Do you mean there is no fixed election-day?"

"None at all," said Philip. "We are always voting. When I left you yesterday afternoon I went in to vote for an alderman of our ward, in place of a man who has resigned. I wish I had taken you in with me, though there was nothing to see. Only three or four great books, each headed with the name of a candidate. I wrote my name in Andrew Second's book. He is, on the whole, the best man. The books will be open three months. No one, of course, can vote more than once, and at the end of that time there will be a count, and a proclamation will be made. Then about removal; any one who is dissatisfied with a public officer puts his name up at the head of a book in the election office. Of course there are dozens of books all the time. But unless there is real incapacity, nobody cares. Sometimes, when one man wants another's place, he gets up a great breeze, the newspapers get hold of it, and everybody is canvassed who can be got to the spot. But it is very hard to turn out a competent officer. If in three months, however, at all the registries, a majority of the voters express a wish for a man's removal, he has to go out. Practically, I look in once a week at that office to see what is going on. It is something as you vote at your clubs."

"Did you say women as well as men?" said I.

"O yes," said Philip, "unless a woman or a man has formally withdrawn from the roll. You see, the roll is the list, not only of voters, but of soldiers. For a man to withdraw, is to say he is a coward and dares not take his chance in war. Sometimes a woman does not like military service, and if she takes her name off I do not think the public feeling about it is quite the same as with a man. She may have things to do at home."

"But do you mean that most of the women serve in the army?" said I.

"Of course they do," said he. "They wanted to vote, so we put them on the roll. You do not see them much. Most of the women's regiments are heavy artillery, in the forts, which can be worked just as well by persons of less as of more muscle if you have enough of them. Each regiment in our service is on duty a month, and in reserve six. You know we have no distant posts."

"We have a great many near-sighted men in America," said I, "who cannot serve in the army."

"We make our near-sighted men work heavy guns, serve in light artillery, or, in very bad cases, we detail them to the police work of the camps," said he. "The deaf and dumb men we detail to serve the military telegraphs. They keep secrets well. The blind men serve in the bands. And the men without legs ride in barouches in state processions. Everybody serves somewhere."

"That is always the reason," said I, with a sigh, "why everybody has so much time in Sybaris!"

Being so much with Kleone, — spending, indeed, an hour quietly at their house, after our school tramp, and before we went to bathe, — I got a chance to ask her about household administration. I did not know whether things did go as easily as they seemed, or whether, as with most households, when strangers are visiting for a time, they seemed to go easier than they did. But I think there cannot be much deception about it. Kleone is not in the least an actress, and she certainly wondered that I thought there could be so much difficulty. She finally took me out into her kitchen, pantry, and so on, and showed me the whole machine.

I do not understand it a great deal better than I did before. But here are a few central facts. First, no washing of clothes is done in any private house. For every thirty or forty families there is one laundry,—λουτρόν they call it; and the people there send twice a week for the soiled linen, and return it clean at the end of forty-eight hours. Kleone said that these establishments were so small that she knew all the workpeople at that near hers; and if she had any special directions to give, she ran in and told what she wanted. Of course they could have all the mechanism they wanted, — large mangles, steam-dryers, folding-machines, and so on. Next, I should think their public baking establishments must be better than ours. Kleone no more thought of making her own bread than my Polly thinks of making her own candles. "I can make it," said she, with a pretty air; "but what 's the good (τῷ καλῷ), when I know they do it as well as I?" For other provant, there is the universal *trattoria* system of all Italy, carried on with the neatness and care of individual right, not to say whim, which I find everywhere here.

I took care to ask specially about servants, and the ease or difficulty of finding and of training them. Here Kleone was puzzled. It was evident she had never thought of the matter at all, any more than she had thought of water-supply, or of who kept the streets clean. But, after a good deal of pumping and cross-questioning, I came at some notion of why this was all so easy. In the first place, there is not a very great amount of what we call menial service to be done in establishments where there are no stairs, no washing, no ironing, no baking, no moving, few lamps to fill, little dusting or sweeping (because all roads and streets here are watered), few errands, and little sickness. But Kleone did not in the least wink out of sight the fact that there was regular service to be done, and that it did not do itself. But, as she said, "as no girl goes to school between fourteen and eighteen, and no boy or girl ever goes to school more than half the time, — as no girl under eighteen or boy under twenty-one is permitted to work in the factories, or indeed anywhere unless at home, — there is an immense force of young folks who must be doing something, and must be trained to do something. You see," said Kleone, "no girl is married before she is eighteen, and perhaps she may not be married before she is twenty-five. From these unmarried women, who are of age after they are eighteen, we may hire servants. And we may receive into our houses girls under that age, if only we exact no duties of them but those of home. Now, if you will think," said she, "in any circle of a hundred people, — say in any family of brothers, sisters, and cousins, — there are enough young people to do all this work you ask about. All we have to do is to exchange a little.

That pretty girl who let you in at the door is a cousin of my husband's who is making a long three months' visit here, — glad to come, indeed, for it is a little quiet, I think, at Trœzene, where her people live. I do not pretend to be a notable housekeeper you know; but if I were, I should have any number of girls' mothers asking me if I would not have them here to stay, and they would do most of my dusting and bed-making for me. Elizabeth, whom I believe you have not seen, is the only person I hire, in the house. She will be married next year, but there are plenty more when she goes."

Speaking of Sophia's letting me in at the door, there is a pretty custom about door-bells. To save you from fumbling round of a dark evening, the bell-pulls are made from phosphorescent wood, or some of them of glass with a glow-worm on a leaf inside, so that you always see this little knob, and know where to put your hand.

The plays were as good and bright as they could be. The theatre is small, but large enough for ordinary voices and ordinary eyes. There are ever so many of them. Then the actors and actresses were these very people whom I have been meeting, or their children, or their friends. The Chief Justice himself took a little part this evening, and that pretty Lydia, his daughter, sang magnificently. She would be a *prima donna assoluta* over at Naples yonder. Father Thomas's daughter is a contralto. She does not sing so well. I do not suppose the Chief is often on the stage; but he was there to-night, just as he might be at a Christmas party in his own house. He said to me, as he walked home with me: "We are not going to let this thing slip into the hands of a lot of irresponsible people. As it stands, it brings the children pleasantly together; and they always have their entertainments where their fathers and mothers do."

A funny thing happened as we left the play. A sudden April shower had sprung up, and so we found the porches and passage-ways lined with close-stacked umbrellas; they looked like muskets in an armory. Every gentleman took one, and those of the ladies who needed. Angelides handed one to me. It seems that the city owns and provides the umbrellas. When I came to the inn, I put mine in the hall, and that was the last I shall see of it. But I have inquired, and it seems that, as soon as the rain is over, the agent for this district will come round in a wagon and collect them. If it rain any day when I am here, a waiter from the inn will run and fetch me one. I shall carry it till the rain is over, and then leave it anywhere I choose. The agent for that district will pick it up, and place it in the umbrella-stand for the nomos. In case of a sudden shower, as this to-night, it is, of course, their business to supply churches or theatres.

I have noticed another good thing about umbrellas. A man in front of me that day it rained had a letter to post at a box which was on a street-lamp. If he had had to hold his umbrella with one hand, — to open the box with another, and to drop in the letter with a third, it would have been awkward, for he had but two hands. So they had made the cover of the box with a ring handle, — he opened it with his umbrella hand, catching the ring with the hook of the umbrella, — and posted his letter with his other hand.

Tuesday, *5th.* — Fine again. I have been with the boys a good deal to-day. They took me to one or two of the gymnasiums, to one of the swimming-schools, to the market for their nomos, and afterwards to an up-town market, to the picture-gallery, *πινακοθήκη*, and museum of yet another nomos, which they thought was finer than theirs, and to their own sculpture-gallery.

As we walked I asked one of them if I was not keeping him from school.

"No," said he, "this is my off-term."

"Pray, what is that?"

"Don't you know? We only go to school three months in winter and three in summer. I thought you did so in America. I know Mr. Webster did. I read it in his Life."

I was on the point of saying that we knew now how to train more powerful men than Mr. Webster, but the words stuck in my throat, and the boy rattled on.

"The teachers have to be there all the time, except when they go in retreat. They take turns about retreat. But we are in two choroi; I am choros-boy now, James is anti-choros. Choros have school in January, February, March, July, August, September. Next year I shall be anti-choros."

"Which do you like best, — off-term or school?" said I.

"O, both is as good as one. When either begins, we like it. We get rather sick of either before the three months are over."

"What do you do in your off-terms?" said I, — "go fishing?"

"No, of course not," said he, "except Strep, and Hipp, and Chal, and those boys, because their fathers are fishermen. No, we have to be in our fathers' offices, we big boys; the little fellows, they let them stay at home. If I was here without you now, that truant-officer we passed just now would have had me at home before this time. Well, you see they think we learn about business, and I guess we do. I know I do," said he, "and sometimes I think I should like to be a Proxenus when I am grown up, but I do not know."

I asked George about this, this evening. He said the boy was pretty nearly right about it. They had come round to the determination that the employment of children, merely because their wages were lower than men's, was very dangerous economy. The chances were that the children were overworked, and that their constitution was fatally impaired. "We do not want any Manchester-trained children here." Then they had found that steady brain-work on girls, at the growing age, was pretty nearly slow murder in the long run. They did not let girls go to school with any persistency after they were twelve or fourteen. After they were twenty they might study what they chose.

"But the main difference between our schools and yours," said he, "is that your teacher is only expected to hear the lesson recited. Our teacher is expected to teach it also. You have in America, therefore, sixty scholars to one teacher. We do not pretend to have more than twenty to one teacher. We do this the easier because we let no child go to school more than half the time; nor, even with the strongest, more than four hours a day.

"Why," said he, "I was at a college in America once, where, with splendid mathematicians, they had had but one man teach any mathematics for thirty years. And he was travelling in Europe when I was there. The others only heard the recitations of those who could learn without being taught."

"I was once there," said I.

.... We bathed in the public bath for this nomos, which is not the same as George's. The boys took me home with them to dine, and George came round here this evening. We have had pleasant talk with some lemon and orange farmers from the country.

I have not said anywhere that their *acquajuoli* are

everywhere in the streets; and a little acid in the water, with plenty of ice and snow, seems to take away the mania for wine or liquor, just as it does in Naples. The temperance of Naples is due, not to the sour wine people talk of, for the laboring men do not drink that, but to the attractive provision made of other drinks. And it is very much so here. These *acquajuoli* are just like those in Naples.

But here no street cuts another at right angles. There is always a curve at the corner, with a chord of a full hundred feet. This enables them to have narrower streets, — no street is more than fifty feet between the sidewalks, — and it gives pretty stands for the fruit-sellers and lemonade-sellers at the quadrants. There is iced water free everywhere, and delicious coffee almost free.

Wednesday, 4th. — As soon as breakfast was over, I went down to Pylades, the boat-builder. I own it, I am distressed to say that he is exactly in time, and the boat, to all purposes, is repaired. She is a much better boat than she ever was before. They know no such thing as a mechanic being an hour late in his performance of a contract. "The man does not know his business, if he cannot tell when he will be done," said Pylades to me. And when I asked what would have happened if his men had not finished this job in time, he shook his head and said "ἁρπαγμός. I should have taken from a citizen what I could not restore, namely, the time you had to wait beyond my promise." I said it was very kind in him to count me as a citizen.

As to that, he said *ξενία*, or the duties of hospitality were even more sacred than those of citizenship; and he quoted the Greek proverb, which I had noticed on the city seal: *Αἰσχύνη πόλεως πολίτῳ ἁμαρτία*,— "The shame of the city is the fault of the citizen."

I cannot see that there is any sort of excuse for my loitering here longer than to-morrow. The paint will be dry and the stores (what a contrast to what I sailed with!) will be on board to-night. Among them all, I believe they will sink her with oranges and cigars, sent as personal presents to me by my friends.

Andrew took me through some of the registration offices. They carry their statistics out to a charm; I could not but think how fascinated Dr. Jarvis would be. But they say, and truly enough, that nothing can be well done in administration unless you know the facts. Take railroads, for instance; if you know exactly how many people are going to come down town from a particular nomos, you can provide for them. But if you do not, they must trust to chance. They know here, and can show you, how many men they have who are twenty-three years and seven days old, or any other age; and every night, of course, they know what is the population of the country in every ward of the whole government.

By appointment, I met the Chief Justice as he adjourned the court, and we rode to the Pier for our last bath. Delicious surf!

I asked him about something which Kleone said, which had surprised me. She said no woman was married till she was eighteen, and that she might not be till she was twenty-five. I did not like to question her; but he tells me everything, and I asked him. He went into the whole history of the matter in his reply, and the system is certainly very curious.

He bade me remember the fundamental importance, as long ago as the laws of Charondas, of marriage in the state. "The unit with us," he said, "is the 'one flesh,' the married man and women. We consider no unmarried man as more than a half, and so with woman." Then he went on to say that they had formerly a hopeless imbroglio of suits, — breach-of-promise cases, divorce cases, cases of gossip, and so on, which had resulted in the present system; and, without quoting words, I will try to describe it. Kleone was right. No woman may marry before she is eighteen. They hold it as certain that, before she is twenty-five, she will have met her destiny. They say that, if no gossip, or manœuvring, or misunderstanding intervene, it is certain that before she is twenty-five, in a simple state of society like this, which places no bar on the free companionship of men and women, the husband appointed for her in heaven will have seen her and made himself known to her. They say that there is no unfair compulsion to his free-will, if they intimate to him that he must do this within a certain time. If it happen that she do not find this man before that age, she must travel away from Sybaris for thirty years, or until she has married abroad. They regard this as exile, which these people, so used to a comfortable life, consider the most horrible of punishments. To tell the truth, I do not wonder. Practically, however, it appears that the punishment is never pronounced. More male children are born into the state than female. This alone indicates that the age of marriage for men must be somewhat higher than that of women. Their custom is, keeping the maximum age of men's marriage at thirty, for the Statistical Board to issue every three months a bulletin, stating what is the minimum age. Just now it is twenty-three years, one month, and eleven days. If a man does not choose to marry here when he is thirty, he spends thirty years in travel, looking for the wife he has not found at home. But, as I say of the women, practically no one goes.

I said that I thought this was a very stern statute, and that it interfered completely with the right of the individual citizen, which they pretend was at the bottom of their system. The Chief Justice said, in reply, that everybody said so. "L'Estrange said so to me in England, and Kleber said so to me in Germany, and Chenowith said so to me in America, and Juarez said so to me in Bolivia. But the truth is, that it is absolutely certain that before a woman is twenty-five, and before a man is thirty, each of them has met his destiny or hers. If the two destinies do not run into one, it is because some infernal gossip, or misunderstanding, or ignorance, or other cause, — I care not what, — intervenes. Now," said he, "you know how hard we are on gossip, since Charondas's time. 'No tale-bearer shall live.' What is left is to see that sentiment, or modesty, or self-denial, or the other curse, as above, shall not intervene to defeat the will of Heaven. For in heaven this thing is done. I can assure you," said he, "that this calm, steady pressure of an expressed determination that people shall carry out their destiny, saves myriads of people from misunderstanding and misery; and that, in practice, no individual right is sacrificed. I know it," he added, after a moment, "for I am the person who must know it. It is not true that all marriages are made here by the Lord Chancellor, — as Dr. Johnson proposed. But it is true that I send into exile the people who will not marry. How many do you think I have exiled, now, in thirteen years?"

I guessed, for a guess' sake, five hundred.

"Not one," said the Chief Justice. "No, nor ever seemed to come near it but once. Every three months there is a special day set apart when the Statistical Board shall send me the lists. For a fortnight before the day there are a great many marriages. When the day comes, I go, Colonel Ingham, into an empty court-room, and sit there for three hours. No officers of court are permitted to be present but myself. Once it happened that when I went in I found a fine young officer, a man whom I knew by sight, sitting there waiting his sentence. I bowed, but said nothing. I took my papers, and asked him if he would come in again at eleven. At half past ten came in a woman whom I had watched since she was a child, — one of those calm, even-balanced people, who are capable of blessing the world, but are so unselfish that they may be pushed one side into washing dishes for beggars. She had her veil down, but walked to the bench, and laid her card before me. I pointed her a seat, and went on with my writing. As the clock struck eleven, I asked her to excuse me for a moment, and I withdrew. I stayed in my private room an hour. I came back at noon, — and my lieutenant-colonel and my queenly Hebe were both gone. It was the victory of a young love. He had worshipped her since they were at school together, and she him. But some tattling aunt — she died just in time to save herself from the galleys — put in some spoke or other, I know not what, that blocked their wheels; she had calmly said "No" to a hundred men, and he had passed like a blind, deaf man among a thousand women. Both of them were ready to go into exile, rather than surrender the true loyalty of youth. But I had the wit to leave them to each other. They were married that afternoon, and all is well!"

AND to-morrow night I shall be jotting my entries here as the sea pitches me up and down in the gulf. When shall I see all these nice friends again? I feel as if I had known them since we were born. I cannot yet analyze the charm. I believe I do not want to. They certainly do not pretend to be saints. They have rather the complete self-respect of people who do not think of themselves at all. The state cares for the citizen, and for nothing else. There is no thought of conquest; nay, they court separation from the world outside. But, on the other hand, the citizen cares for the state, — seems to see that he is lost if this majestic administration is not watching over him and defending him. Because the law guards their individual rights, even their individual caprices, there is certainly less tyranny of Mrs. Grundy and of fashion. But yet I never lived among people who had so little to say about their own success, — about "I said," "I told him," or "my way," or "I told my wife."

When I spoke to the chief the other day of their homage to individual right, he said they made the citizen strong because they would make the state strong, and made the state strong that it might make the citizen strong. I quoted Fichte: "The human race is the individual, of which men and women are the separate members." "Fichte got it from Paul," said he. "If you mean to have a sound mind in a sound body, you must have a sound little finger and a clear eye.

But you will not have a clear eye, or a sound little finger, unless you have a sound mind in a sound body. Colonel Ingham, — Love is the whole!"

It has been a pretty bleak evening. I have been running round with George to say good by. Kleone asked me, so prettily, when I would come with *Μαριάδιον*. It was half a minute before I reflected that *Μαριάδιον* is Greek for Polly!

Thursday, *3d Kal. Θαργηλ.* — At the boat at 8.30. The old man was there without the boys. He said they wanted to stay here.

"Among the devils?" said I.

The old man confessed that the place for poor men was the best place he ever saw; the markets were cheap, the work was light, the inns were neat, the people were civil, the music was good, the churches were free, and the priests did not lie. He believed the reason that nobody ever came back from Sybaris was, that nobody wanted to.

The Proxenus nodded, well pleased.

"So Battista and his brother would like to stay a few months; and he found he might bring Caterina too, when my Excellency had returned from Gallipoli; or did my Excellency think that, when Garibaldi had driven out the Bourbons, all the world would be like Sybaris?"

My Excellency hoped so; but did not dare promise.

"You see now," said George, "why you hear so little of Sybaris. Enough people come to us. But you are the only man I ever saw leave Sybaris who did not mean to return."

"And I," said I, — "do you think I am never coming here again?"

"You found it a hard harbor to make," said the Proxenus. "We have published no sailing directions since St. Paul touched here, and those which he wrote — he sent them to the Corinthians yonder — neither they nor any one else have seemed to understand."

"Good by."

"God bless you! Good by." And I sailed for Gallipoli.

Wind N. N. W., strong. I have been pretty blue all day. And the old man is too. It is just 7.30 P. M. The lights of the Castle of Otranto are in sight, and I shall turn in. *Χαῖρε.*

HOW THEY LIVED AT NAGUADAVICK.

FROM REV. FREDERIC INGHAM'S PAPERS.

I.

NAGUADAVICK was in itself, of nature, like any other town, only a good deal worse. I mean that the lake took up all one side of it, so nobody could live there. Then on the river front nobody would live if he could. Out on the roads to Assabet and Plimquoddy you could get no water that anybody would drink. So it happened that in the town proper everybody had to live on the north side. This made land there dear, and would have made rents very high if we had not found out a much better way to live, — of which I am now going to give you the history.

"In balloons?"

Not a bit of it. There is no word of nonsense in what I am going to tell you. It is only a thing perfectly practicable in every spirited American town which needs it, and the only wonder is that it was not done in every such town long ago. It has been tried for, everywhere, in a fashion, and it only needs brains, and enterprise, and faith in men, to carry it out everywhere with success.

It all began at a meeting of their Union. "Trade's

Union?" Not exactly. In a Trade's Union only one trade meets. This was a meeting of all sorts of people, with trades and without, with money and without, — some with one idea and some with seven, — a union which they used to have in a decent sort of club-house they had. Men and women could go, and did. You played checkers, or euchre, or billiards, — or you went up stairs and danced, — or you read in the reading-room, or you talked in the drawing-room. And in the committee-room there was almost every evening what they called a Section, where something or other was up, — maybe a tableau, maybe a debating-club, maybe a paper on the legs of cockchafers. They called it all the "Union for Christian Work." Well, one night in the committee-room they had had rather a dreary powwow about the future of Naguadavick. Pretty much all of them agreed Naguadavick was going to the dogs. They could not raise pineapples, and it was evidently unhealthy for cats. All the merchants went to Boston for their spring and fall supplies, instead of buying them of each other. The manufacture of horn gun-flints had proved successful, but they cost more when they were made than the stone ones; and, worst of all, as I have remarked, there was no chance for anybody to live anywhere, if the population of the town should enlarge by one. For every house was occupied, and it was known to the presiding officer that at Mrs. Varnum's boarding-house, the mistress had that day refused to receive a family from out of town because they had eleven children.

So it was generally agreed that Naguadavick was going to the dogs as fast as it could go. I never was in but one thoroughly prosperous town that was not, if you could trust the talking kind.

Meanwhile, in fact, Naguadavick was a driving, thriving, striving, hiving, wiving, and living town of 23,456 people by the last United States census, with "probably at the present time rising 36,000, if only the beggarly and miserly city council had not refused to take a special count when they levied the tax last spring."

Ogden went home from that meeting red-hot, he was so mad. He told his wife all they had said, and said he could not stand it. She said she should not think he could. He said it was all nonsense. She said it certainly was, but she wished he would not swear so. He said he would not again, but it was enough to make the minister swear and burn his books too. She said she hoped the minister would not burn Consuelo till she had a chance to finish it. This made Ogden laugh, — it was old Elkanah's nephew; did you know him? and they went to bed. But Ogden was thoroughly mad this time; he said he would not stand it, and he would not have any more such talk at the Union. And he did not. They have talked nonsense there since. But they never talked this same nonsense. And this was the way he managed it.

As soon as he had read his letters the next morning at the mill, and had just walked through all the rooms, (Ogden made whips for export, — Boothia Felix, — immense demand for sea-horses,) he told his boy he should be out for two hours, went across to the offices of the Great Eastern Railway, and charged right in on Greenleaf. Capital fellow, Greenleaf, the best man, I think, and the most spirited and most spiritual, and the most to be loved, of all men I have ever known. Greenleaf had done his letters too; — had seen all his heads of department, — and he put down the Advertiser, — gave Ogden two chairs, — and put his feet in one.

"Why did you not stay in the Section Room, last night?" said Ogden.

"You know," said Greenleaf. "Why — *did* you?"

"Why indeed," said Ogden again, "unless to see how far the infernal tomfoolery of croaking may lead men. It seems to be literally and really supposed that these people, who have known enough to dam this river, where there is a quicksand bottom, — who know enough to make fine sewing-thread in air so dry that it sparkles, — who know enough to split a flint into ten thousand million billion flinders no bigger than the mustache of a mosquito, — don't know how to live, and will go off to Death's Hollow, because the boarding-houses are full. Jove! Why don't they send us all back to the Lincolnshire Fens and to —

what you call it — old Brewster's place, Ansterfield — Scrooby — in the edge of York, to-morrow! Why, the monkeys know more, for they know enough, if they can't live in one place, to live in another!"

Thus far, remembering his wife's warning, Ogden went on, and sinned not with his tongue, nor weakened the force of what he said, by any profane exaggeration.

Greenleaf laughed, and said he had not heard so much twaddle as he heard in the five minutes he was there, and Ogden was much comforted.

So soothed, he began again. "Now, Frank, I want to stop all this. If it goes on, it may do serious injury. In the first place, such talk will ruin the Union. Who is going there if that whining, canting, drivelelling old fool is going to talk such stuff? What 's worse is, it will get into the papers. They would not put it in the Spy; but old Martin at the Courant is just ass enough to put in something about the decline of our population, and the unhealthy condition of the muskrats who live under the long dike. I had to go round there this morning to stop him off this time. Well, of course, nobody reads their trash; but, after they have put it in a few million times, it gets copied somewhere, and it sticks, and then people will really think this place has gone up, and not an owl or a jackal will come here to rear jackets or owlets!"

"Who is croaking now?" said Greenleaf, laughing. "You did not come here to say that."

" No," said Ogden, standing up, " I did not." And he walked to the large scale map of the Great Eastern road. " I came here to show you this." And he pointed out a spot eleven miles from Naguadavick, on the line of that road. " What could you buy the Lemon property here for ? "

" House and land, — there are four hundred acres ; I suppose thirty-five thousand dollars would be the asking price."

" Yes, — and out here, — the Gregory place ? "

Greenleaf said that was not worth so much. There was more land, but it was poor land, and the house had been burned down. Ogden said he did not care how poor the land was, and he sat down again.

" Tell your directors to buy those two places to-morrow. If you have not got any money, issue some bonds and get some. Open a new station where the Sudbury road crosses yours. Cut up the nine hundred acres into lots of a quarter-acre, a half-acre, and an acre, say, in all, two thousand lots. These lots will cost you rather less than fifty dollars apiece, on the average. Fix the price of each lot on your lithograph plan, and never vary from it. Then advertise that for twenty years you will run special trains in, from your new station, at 6, 6.30, and 7 in the morning, and as many more as you choose, — that you will run them out at 6, 6.30, 7, and 8 in the evening, and as many more as you choose. Not one train shall stop on the way, — and every man shall be in town in twenty-two minutes from the time he started. Before you are five years older, if you keep your promises, that station will do a business of two thousand tickets a day, each way. In ten years its business will be five thousand tickets. And your rascally railroad will be blest of men and angels as a corporation with a soul."

Greenleaf laughed, — and locked the door. Then he opened a large drawer. "Look here," said he. "When I left you, last night, I came home here and drew out this plan, not for the Lemon place, but for the Chenery farm, which is better. We may take the Gregory property if we like. I have seen the chief, and he says, 'Go ahead.' He says he will take it on his own shoulders, — that the company may not like to carry it long enough. He says he shall lose nothing on the investment, and that it will bring up his stock. And so it will.

"We shall put the lots at twice what they cost us, for there must be a sure profit, and we shall sell them as the Illinois Central sells lots, ten per cent down and ten per cent each year for ten years, on our asking price, without other interest. The company guarantees, as you say, fast trains for twenty years. That will make room for ten thousand people, Elk."

Elkanah was very much pleased, and they went into the detail. His two hours went by very fast, and then he went away. When he had been five minutes gone, Greenleaf sent for him. "Ogden," said he,

" don't you think you had better get up a little earlier in the morning the next time you advise this road ?" Ogden was good-natured, and stood the chaff like a man.

II.

As soon as Greenleaf had bought the Chenery farm, and got a bond for a deed of the Gregory property, if he wanted it, he published the details of his plan.

Of course all the croakers were sure it would fail. It had been tried ten thousand times, they said, and had failed. " Canton, East Boston, Mount Bellingham, Hyde Park," said the croakers, who knew nothing at all about the success or failure of either of these enterprises, " when did not this plan fail ? People won't go where you want to send them."

" Tell me," said Greenleaf, cheerfully, — he was the only man worth anything who never got mad by any accident, — and this, as above, because he was so spirited and spiritual at once, — " tell me, when this ship has not sailed, if she was built before she was launched ? I have heard of old Dutchmen, who built the forecastle of a ship, and launched it, and it went to the bottom, — and of cousins of theirs who built the stern first, and launched that, — and were surprised that it did not sail ten knots an hour. So, I have heard of people who laid out cities on paper for their own advantage, — and forgot the advantage of their settlers. And I have heard of railroads who opened stations where no people lived, — and then sold no tickets. I have heard of new towns opened at way stations, — and people did not choose to churn along in snuffy old accommodation trains. But I have never heard of a place where a man was sure of four fast trains every morning and four more every night, that did not fill up in no time."

Down at the Union, one night, Ogden got talking about the new place, and somebody told him the Parisians would not sleep out of Paris. "No," said he, "nor will the people of this place sleep outside of Naguadavick, if sleeping outside means that they are to have no fun out there. If there are to be no parties, no theatre, no concert, no Union, no chance to croak together, nobody is going to live there. That is another reason why you must begin on a large scale. You must have people enough to make it worth Greenleaf's while to run four fast trains for you, morning and evening. If you have them, you will have people enough to persuade Blitz to juggle for you, Mrs. Wood to sing to you, Wendell Phillips and Henry Beecher to lecture for you, and the French company to act for you. The people who will go to this place to live are exactly the sort of people who will put all that thing through. You will have a better public hall there than we have got here." And so, indeed, it proved.

I was at that time the minister of the Sandemanian church at Naguadavick. I believed in Greenleaf, and indeed I rather believed in this thing. So I went round one day and asked him if they did not mean to reserve lots for churches, and if they would not let me secure one. "Look at the plan, Mr. Ingham," said Greenleaf. "You will see some red crosses there on half-acre lots, which will be convenient for churches."

I looked, compared, and called his attention to one which seemed to me the best. I said I did not know if we could or would do anything about it, but would they not give us a deed of that lot, on condition we would use it for a house of worship.

"We will give you a deed," said Greenleaf, "on exactly the same terms as we would give the government one for a post-office. Those terms you will find in brief on the plan. That lot is worth one hundred and twenty dollars, and for that sum the Sandemanian Consistory can have it. Look here, Mr. Ingham," said he, "religion, as I understand it, is the most essential reality in earth or in heaven. The institutions of religion then, as churches or Sunday schools, will in no wise put themselves on the plane of inferior organizations, as if they must beg for a living or for right to be. They will assert their right. We shall treat all institutions of religion with precisely equal respect. And I believe that the Sandemanians will find it desirable to buy a lot here now, while they can, to build by and by, when they want to."

I told him he was quite right; that the Sandemanian church, at least, was in no position to ask alms like a beggar. And so the next Sunday morning I spoke of the thing from the pulpit. I said it seemed to me we ought to secure a lot there, before the most available situations were taken up by others. I said that any money I found in the charity boxes that evening after the two services, would be applied to this purpose. And, as it happened, I found one hundred and nineteen dollars and nineteen cents there. Polly had eighty-one cents lying by, which she added, and we bought the lot the next morning. A very curious thing followed. The Spy and the Courant mentioned this fact, and, before a fortnight was over, the Unitarians, and the Universalists, and the Methodists, and Free Will Baptists, and Orthodox Congregationalists, and Baptists, and Episcopalians, and even Roman Catholics, had each bought lots. "They did not mean," they said, "to have those proselyting Sandemanians stepping in before them." So there seemed to be no danger but Aboo-Goosh, as they called the new town, would have enough religious privileges.

III.

ELKANAH OGDEN talked so much about the "Suburb of Ease" at the Union, and in all social circles, he explained away so many difficulties, and pooh-poohed down so many objections, that he came to be considered as a sort of godfather to the plan ; and all sorts of people consulted him about it. After the lithographic plans were printed by the Great Eastern, and the demand for their house-lots became very spirited, people began to wake up who had been very drowsy before, or had said it was all nonsense, and that nothing could ever come of it. And all sorts of contrivers came to Ogden with their plans, and bored him awfully.

Among others there came in one day an old farmer, whom Ogden did not know from Adam. But he supposed he had seen him before; so he said, "Good morning, Mr. Jones. Take a chair."

But the old man said, "My name is not Jones. I live next the Jones farm. My name is Tenny, Elbridge Tenny. I live out in Knox."

Elkanah apologized.

Then the old man said that he had come to talk to him about his place. It was a beautiful farm, he said, sloping down each side of the north branch, which ran right through the place. Putting his father's place and his together, and throwing in the jointure property, there was nigh seven hundred acres in all. By this time Ogden understood that here was another man who would like to sell by the foot what had been bought by the acre.

"You see," said the old man, "if you want horse-cars, the grade is beautiful from each side down to the Great Northern Road, and the flat, where the stream bends, is just the place for a station."

"I dare say, Mr. Jones," said Ogden. "I beg your pardon, Mr. Eldridge, I dare say. But all this depends on what the 'Great Northern' says. I have never found them very bright, or, which is much the same thing, very humane."

Mr. Tenny said his name was not Eldridge, and Ogden apologized again. Tenny had not been to the Great Northern people; he had begun by drawing out his plan for streets, which perhaps Ogden would like to see. And then he had thought he would come and consult Mr. Ogden before he went any further.

"Well, sir," said Elkanah, "I am very much obliged to you. Now I tell you that your farm may be as beautiful as the Garden of Eden, and as well laid out as Alexander's city in Egypt, but unless the Great Northern does the right thing, which is to say the handsome thing, you can do nothing with the farm in this way. More than that, Mr. Tenny [this time he was quite correct], more than that, they may be as handsome as — as — the Chevalier Crichton, and if you, up there, are the least bit short-sighted, or try to skin these workingmen whom you want to plant there, the whole thing fails again. As I have said forty times, the enterprise is one combined enterprise, which seeks everybody's good. It seeks the good of the honest day-laborer, who is now paying a dollar a week for his tenement here, it seeks the good of his children not yet born, it seeks the good of the Great Northern Railroad and all its stockholders, and it seeks your good. But if any one of the parties undertakes to overreach any of the others, the whole thing fails, and deserves to fail."

By this time Ogden was unduly excited, and Mr. Tenny was a little alarmed. But he declared that he felt all this also, and only wanted to make a reasonable profit in the business, which he was willing everybody else concerned should share. Ogden cooled down, and told him that the merit of the enterprise was that it offered, not fabulous profit to anybody, but a perfectly steady and sure remuneration, — steady and sure, as he proposed to show. So they walked over together to the house of the president of the Great Northern. It was afternoon, and they knew he would not be at the office. They also knew that in that establishment responsibility was very badly divided, and that he would take it very ill if any such proposal as this were made to any of his subordinates before he had heard of it. In fact, if he could be persuaded, before the week were over, that he had devised the whole thing, that would be best of all.

It was very slow work, and, to a person as impetuous as Elkanah, very tedious. But he kept his temper like a saint, knowing how much depended on that. He let the president ramble off into endless histories of his own former successes in dealings with lumbermen, with politicians, and with owners of water-power, — in all of which, he, being the painter of the picture, came off victorious, and these several lions crouched at his feet. After many of these rambles into the forests of facts gilded by memory, he said, well pleased: —

"Then your object is to persuade us to open a new station at the Bates Crossing? We might perhaps let the milk-trains stop there,— and the Montaigne special. How would that answer? That would give you two trains in winter, and three in summer each way."

Elbridge Tenny looked round dubersome on Elkanah Ogden, and this time Elkanah blazed away.

"It would not answer at all, Mr. Chauncey. This is one of those enterprises, where you must do everything or nothing. The railroads of this part of the country have steadily cut off their best revenue, — the most reliable because not subject to competition, — by that policy of leaving their suburb travel to their accommodation trains. Unless we can have at least three morning expresses and three in the evening, we can do nothing."

It was a wonder Mr. Chauncey did not faint away, or show them the door as madmen. But Ogden had expected, even had intended, this surprise.

"The people who are to come and go on these trains, Mr. Chauncey," said he, "are not women going a shopping, to whom ten minutes more or less is of no account. They are not even bank clerks, or dry-goods dealers, to whom all is gained if they are on the street here at nine in the morning. We want to provide for the day-laborer, who must get to his work at eight in the winter and at seven in the summer. We mean to have him, and his employer, as certain that he will be there, as if he had only to walk, in fifteen minutes from his home. You cannot give him that certainty, if he must wait till your Montaigne train has made its connections above, and come down to Bates's. Besides this, we want to promise him a seat sure, — while he goes and while he comes. He must not be dependent on the chances of your up-travel. And when he takes his nap, — if he chooses to, riding out, — he is not to be waked at six or eight way stations. He is to be put through."

Mr. Chauncey smiled, — sublime, amused, and incredulous. But the smile faded when Ogden proceeded: "These fast trains are promised by the Great Eastern for the next twenty years, to people who take lots at Aboo Goosh, and that is the reason that they have already sold seven hundred lots. Offer nothing but way trains, stopping at all your near stations, and Mr. Tenny here need take no trouble about surveying his lands. He will not sell five acres!"

The President became more thoughtful at this. "Have you thought what you should offer us?" said he; "what bonus would be reasonable to induce us to try the experiment? We might put on one express for three months, and see how it would work."

"And you would not have passengers enough to pay for your oil," replied Elkanah. "No, Mr. Chauncey, it is a twenty years' business, or it is nothing, that we propose to you. There is nobody now at Bates's but Mr. Eldridge here, and he and his family will not want many tickets. This business is to be made. When it is made, it is sure."

"And what inducement do you suggest?" said the President again, blandly.

"Simply what I have named. Mr. Eldridge here will be glad to sell you land for your station, at exactly the same price that he will sell me mine for my cottage, or the Widow Conley for hers. On the other hand, if he sells his two thousand lots, and sees his two thousand houses go up in the next ten years, you can guess how many tickets you will sell daily."

"But they are tickets sold at a reduced price," persisted Mr. Chauncey. "I hate these excursions!"

"Pardon me," said Ogden, "there is no reason why you should put them at a reduced price. Put them at the price that will pay you best on the whole. Only announce the price before Mr. Tenny [name right this time] puts a surveyor on the land, and never change it for twenty years. The system is everything."

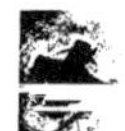

"Where is not the system everything?" said the President, pleased with himself for saying something. And he promised to think of it carefully, for in three hours he had really got interested in the prospects the plan unfolded, and his visitors withdrew.

Two days after, Mr. Chauncey went down to the office and had a long talk with Plinlimmon, his superintendent, and Pariss, his treasurer. Plinlimmon was fretting to death, as he heard from day to day about Aboo Goosh, and thought what golden chances the Great Northern was losing. But he knew it would be madness for him to broach any such plan. Imagine his relief when, after infinite preface and explanation, Mr. Chauncey told him how he had been long wishing that they might build up a local business of their own, so that they should not be so dependent on those cut-throats of the Mad River line and the Canadian connection; how he had turned over many plans, and finally had concluded that if they established a station with several fast trains, say at Bates's cross-roads, they might build up really a large town there; how he had talked with that Mr. Tenny, whom they had to compromise with, about the land at the Sias cutting, and found him well disposed to such an undertaking; and in short, how he, Chauncey, had now come down to talk it over with him, Plinlimmon, and him, Pariss, and if he, Pariss, and he, Plinlimmon, saw no objections, which did not occur to him, Chauncey, he, Chauncey, believed he should send Mr. Stephenson up to make a little survey, and should bring it before the Board the next Monday. The two young men were immensely interested, immensely sympathetic, asked very intelligent questions, proposed very modest objections, and were then driven from these objections; and by the time Mr. Chauncey left them, he was satisfied that he had planned the village of

Rosedale, at least five years ago. He had left its name to Mrs. Chauncey, and this was her selection.

As for our other railroad, — the Cattaraugus and Katahdin, — it never occurred to anybody to suggest anything to any of their people ; and they have never had a fast special train from that hour to this, nor ever will. The only thoroughly original thing they ever did was to pay in currency in Naguadavick the interest they had promised to pay in gold in London.

IV.

It was astonishing to see these two towns grow. You see it was not the ordinary speculation of selling house-lots to other people, while you do not go yourself to live there. But both towns were based on that ingenious Vineland principle. It is the principle on which Uncle Sam sells his farm-lots at the West. The price of the lots, once established, was established forever, so far as the first holder went. Of course they became more valuable every day. Of course every man who bought one whispered to his next friend that there was an admirable chance next him, if he only seized at once. Everybody tried to seize at once, and Aboo Goosh and Rosedale were soon alive with the hum of the hammer and the buzz of the mortising-machine. By the time we dedicated the Sandemanian church at Aboo Goosh, and that was really as soon as we could get up a respectable church edifice, there were five hundred houses inhabited there. In two years more there were two thousand.

Anybody will understand how the people with comfortable incomes lived there. That sort of people live outside the towns they work in everywhere. London, Boston, New York, all places of size, let the men who receive salaries, and who begin to work at nine in the morning, live in their suburbs, — and they all know how to provide for that class of people. The good fortune of Naguadavick was, that in these Aboo Goosh and Rosedale enterprises, we provided for the day-laborers also. The people who worked in the mills, the mere diggers and builders, who had to stand in rows to be hired on the blind side of the Phenix Bank, opposite the Common, the women who sewed in the cloak-shops, — all found it cheapest and best to live in the country, and to do their work in town.

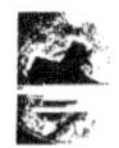

I had myself to leave Naguadavick when these towns had been four years under way. I left it for no fault on either side, but in consequence of an unfortunate misunderstanding and *emeute* at a public meeting, called for the purpose of teaching the children to hold their knives better at table. But up till that time I was intimate in both these new towns. And I may close this account of them with the notes of my last visit in Rosedale.

I called there on an old parishioner of mine, named Mary Quinn. She hailed originally from Carrick on Suir, but had married Michael Quinn, who was from a village just outside of Tipperary, some years before I knew her. She had six or eight children here, and two in heaven. I hunted her up in Rosedale, — found her a mile from the station, on the horse-railroad. They had a regular system of horse-railroad tracks there, that virtually passed every man's house. There was a nice garden round the house, of half an acre, — no fence, which seemed odd; but there was hardly a fence in Rosedale. They had some side hedges, but made up for stronger fences by strict cattle laws. The house itself was a clever story-and-a-half house, such as costs in a country town five hundred dollars. I found this had cost Quinn rather more than seven hundred. The lot had cost him seventy-five. He had paid for that clear, with money he had in bank. He and his wife had paid a third part of the cost of the house, and there was a mortgage on it of four hundred and sixty dollars. Their Savings Bank there took such mortgages, if they knew the people. The truth was, that the land was worth now ten times what the original price was.

"Well, Mrs. Quinn," said I, "I am glad to see the little girl so nicely."

The child, when I saw her last, in one of our back streets, had been white and puny, worrying along with the relics of scarlet fever. She was now rugged, sunburned, freckled, and looked as if she would like to eat a tenpenny nail.

"Indade she is, your Riverince, and it is hard to

say why, for the medicines are all gone, and we have not sent for the new doctor, since we came here."

This was a stroke of humor on Mrs. Quinn's part. She knew well enough that her children were growing up to a constitution like her own, because they were growing up in the same way as she did.

"But the boys, your Riverince, they are the handsomest sight, if you could only see them. They 're all gone now for blackberries, — or for I don't know what, for indeed the fields here are not like what we had at Carrick on Suir, — but they are grown so big and so brown that you would not know them."

"And how does there come enough to eat, if they are so big and hungry ?"

"There, again," said she, with the pride with which the hunter praises his hounds, and the farmer his grounds, and the bishop his lawn. She flung open the door of the neat kitchen we were sitting in, and pointed to the well-hoed potato-patch behind the house, and to the rows of comely cabbages behind them, — as if she had compassed sea and land, lived at the Five Points and in North Street, and now in Back-street-court-place in Naguadavick, not in vain, if she could only have her own potatoes at the last. Of them she said nothing; but, with that speaking wave of the hand which would have become Rachel herself: "And the milk, your Riverince, which cost us ten cents a quart in town, is only six cents here. Half the neighbors have cows, and it is handier for them to let my

boys milk for them, and pay them in milk, than to hire for money. For they don't all have boys as fine as mine," said Mary, who had her weak points, like the rest of us. "For butcher's meat we have more than ever, and it costs us less. Two pigs my man brought up last year on the place here, and though they said the pork was not the fattest, it made a big place in the bill any way, for the butcher allowed us all it was worth, or he said he did, and surely that was a good deal more than nothing."

Then I cross-questioned Mary about their social life, tried to make her own that she felt the want and the excitements and amusements open to her in Back-street-court-place; but there was no craving for their flesh-pots. Pretty clearly, her "man" was more of a man here, and she was more of a woman. Why? Why, because they held Real Estate. Real very emphatic, and with a very large R, — and Estate with a very large E. What is it Jupiter ordains? I am writing at No. 9, in the 3d range, and must quote from memory: —

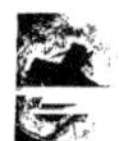

> "The day
> That makes a man a slave takes half his life away."

Well, he might have added, if it were he, and I believe it was not, he might have added: —

> "When he can
> Say, 'This lot of land is mine,' he 's twice a man."

There is no need to be sentimental about it, but that is the living fact. The glory of New England as she was, was that every man was a freeholder.

"My man," said Mary, affecting not to boast, but really running over with pride, "my man does not have much time for the garden. He just cuts at the trees a little, and looks at the boys' work, and taches them a little about the pig; but after supper he has to dress himself and go to the meeting of the co-operative store, where he is a manager, or he sings in the bass in the International Club, or he takes his turn on the sanitary committee of the Union." Poor Mike, too, then, he had come to enjoy the sweets of "eventful living," and his wife had come to the pride of having her husband "sought-arter," second only to the pride of being "sought-arter" herself, in the not forgotten days of seventeen.

Boys and girls both might now be trusted out-doors; and out-doors was a joy and delight to their mother as to them. There was no longer the horrid watch and anxiety there had been in the wynds and courts of the city. Every summer the large market farmers who surrounded them at Rosedale were glad enough to hire the children on jobs to pick peas and beans and the small fruits; and, in fact, we got our vegetables the better in the city market, because we had sent, not an ornamental, but a working population, to our suburbs. It was their gain and it was ours too.

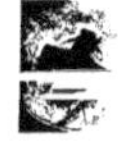

Mary's grandest moment was when she asked me to tea. When I got up to go she said with a reality far beyond any of the tones of artificial civility, that I must stay to see the children and take a cup of tea.

In Back-street-court-place she would have welcomed me had I looked into the crowded kitchen parlor bedroom at tea-time, but, had I come in before tea-time she would no more have asked me to stay than she would have asked me to hear her square the hypothenuse. But now I should not see the children, nor Mike, she said, unless I stayed to tea. And she was sure I should be late at home, which was true; and I was glad I stayed, because I saw the children, which was best of all.

In they came, clattering and explaining, — the youngest first, by some miraculous law, then two or three of the biggest, then a miscellaneous assortment, wound up with him, always the last, who had on this occasion got into the brook, and brought in his shoes in his hand. Clattering and enthusiastic were all the party, each telling his part of the story on a somewhat high key, and all explaining about the quantity and quality of the berries, which were indeed manifold. Mary sympathized, applauded, wondered, and quieted, tried to bring them to consciousness that the old minister was there, promised that they should have the blackberries for tea and for breakfast, bade Phelim and Owen go quick for the milk, whispered to Mary Ann that she was to run to the baker's and buy some tea-cakes, and bade the others go quick to their rooms and wash themselves and brush their hair that they might be ready.

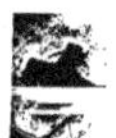

Their rooms! Why did not she say their thrones

or their palaces? Heavens! had not I seen all those children lying asleep together in one room, fifteen feet by twelve, in which all the cooking of that family had been done that day, — all Mrs. Aminidab Johnson's family washing done, — and in which the white muslin dress that Selina Johnson wore to a birthday ball the next night was ironed while those children slept, so that Phelim and Owen might carry it home in the morning? Such, dear reader, is the stowage in every Back-street-court-place within half a mile of where you read these lines! Their rooms, indeed!

"And come into the sitting-room yourself, 'your Riverince,'" continued Mary. "I would have asked you in before, but it seems more sociable here, and more like old times." Nor had she reason to apologize for her well-blacked Banner, her neat kitchen table, and brilliant tin ware, nor for the pretty garden view before which I had been sitting. But I went into the sitting-room, knowing I must be out of the way now while she "got tea."

Reader, I have taken tea with that same woman's sister Margaret in the cabin both were born in, outside Carrick on Suir. It was a stone cabin with a mud floor; a partition of board partly separated us from the pig, who had the front of the doorway, but who was visible to the inquiring eye. I made my call at twilight, and found Mary's nieces and nephews seated on low blocks, or on their heels, looking in the fire of peat. One of them ran for Margaret, to whom I had come to bring a message, three thousand miles from Mary. Instantly, when she appeared, had a troop of ravens been sent out to borrow tea and sugar, that I might feast; instantly had two oat-cakes been set up against the stones on the hearth; soon had the kettle boiled and the tea been ready, and then we had all repaired into Margaret's bedroom, — size, as I live, six feet by five, — my Reverence carrying with me the only chair in the house, while John the husband sat on the bed, while the teapot and oat-cake smoked at the little table, and Margaret, having in fact nothing to sit upon, stood and served. That grandeur of one chair, borrowed tea, and a barefoot life by a peat-fire was what this Mary Quinn was born to. Yes, and for my notion, I think it was better for her and her brothers and sisters than the tenement life, upper story, three flights, in Back-street-court-place, where the children feasted and slept in the corners left by Mrs. Johnson's and Selina's spotless drapery. But to be ushered out by this same Mary, not into the five-foot-six bedroom, to feast from a groaning taper-stand, but into the comely sitting-room, — with its six painted chairs, its sofa and ornamented centre-table (shade of St. Patrick), its portraits of Dan O'Connell, Theobald Mathew, George Washington on his death-bed, and framed testimony of membership of the Siloam Division; to see the cheer and joy with which that woman remembered that she was not living either in a pig-sty or in a barrack, and the sweet saintliness with which she thanked God that she was not; — to see this, and to know this, and to remember this, was to make Rosedale glow indeed with the true roseate hue. I should not have selected the pictures or furniture, but she had. They were her taste, if not mine, and there was the glory. "Excuse me for a moment," said the matron, "Honora will be down stairs presently," and retired, intent on hospitable cares. I had enough to think of to make it unnecessary for me to read the last Harper, or Mr. Hoadley's "Genghis Khan and his Coadjutors." I only had the Harper in my hand that I might not seem neglected when my pretty little Honora came in.

And that was really the same child whom I had seen faded and dead in the alley-ways of the town! She remembered the things she said then, and had the book Polly gave her then for a Christmas present. The same child? What one thing in her was the same? This nut-brown face against that limy-white skin, these hard round arms against those skinny fagots of muscle and tendon, this modest, simple look, against that eager, inquiring, dissatisfied, anxious glare! And when I talked with her, — (the child knew me as well as she knew her father,) — when I talked with her, here were undertakings, and friends, books, walks, collections of butterflies, a party to Mount Greenback, a picnic at Paradise, — all this, against the stupid town life of such a child, who has gone to school and come back if she is good, and gone again and come back again; but to whom one day has been as another, because her mother cannot trust her much in the streets, and there is for her no possibility of society in its forms of simple, light-hearted pleasure! Dear reader, if you care to go into Back-street-court-place in Boston or in New York, you may find as many hundred Honoras as you choose, who never saw the sea on the beach, never picked shell from sand, never planted seed in ground, never watched bird's nest on tree, never crunched moss with foot, never sailed chip on stream, never hunted butterfly over grass, never rested under shady tree, never waded across mountain brook, never picked berry from bough, never ate peach or pear, never rode on horse or ass, never sat in wagon or sleigh, never enjoyed one of the little pleasures which are as the daily food of your children, which they think of so little that they are begging you to-day for something more, because these are things of course to everybody.

So, you see, Honora was herself the heroine of a romance to me. There is the reason why I read so few novels, dear boy; it is because I see so many. And here comes in the great shy Frederic, — my Riverince's godson, — who has endued himself rapidly in his Sunday jacket because of my staying to tea, and who is shy and ill at ease both because I am there and because he has on the jacket. But I administer a story of the good fortune of Dick McKelvy, who has gone to Mexico with the army, and I show Fred a burning-glass of a pattern he has never seen, and he becomes communicative. Can it be possible! This godson, who was erst a little wild, you must know, — who really, if you will not mention it, got into the lock-up one day because he threw marbles at an auctioneer, and, which was ten thousand times worse, at the common law, slapped the policeman who tried to stop him, — this godson, for whom I then and there had to go bail that he should keep the peace of the State, else he would have been sent to the house of correction, — this wild godson of mine is the most sedate, if the most enterprising of human beings. He has formed alliance, offensive and defensive, with Hod Bates (Hod is short for Horace). "You know Hod Bates?" My Reverence had not that pleasure. "Well, Hod is a first-rate fellow, and his father owns a saw-mill up at Number Nine and two townships in the Seventh, and Hod is going up with the men next winter to take care of one of the camps, and he has asked his father to let me go up and take care of the other; and if he likes and I like, I am to have a chance at the mill when it begins running in April, — the fellow that is there now is going to Illinois," &c., &c., &c. Fred is on a larger stage now, and the accumulated steam which erst fired marbles, as from a Perkins gun, on my excellent friend Cunningham with his hammer, is now to drive the mill which is to cut the plank, which is to lay the floor of the court-house, in which you, my dear Frisbie, are to lay down the law which is to save from ruin these States in all coming time! This is the house that Fred built!

A slight commotion, and it is announced that Mike's train passes the window. Ten minutes more (for the horse-cars are not Metropolitan, let us be thankful) and Mike's step is heard at the side door. Two minutes for a second wash, for brushing the hair even with Methodistical precision, and for a Sunday coat, and Mike emerges into the sitting-room. His ride out of town has been his visit to his club-room; he has picked up all the gossip of Naguadavick and of Rosedale. He tells me more news than I have heard in a week, and does the honors with infinite volubility. Thirty seconds more and Mary's tea-bell rings. That Mary Quinn should need a tea-bell! that the little hawks are not sitting on their perches waiting to descend on the visible meal! And we go in to sit, not on the bed of her bedroom, but in the neat kitchen, at her pretty table, where everything, dear Amphitryon, is served a great deal hotter from the stove than you will ever have it in your palace, for all your patent contrived double dishes and covers, and for all your very noisy dumb-waiters.

On that hospitable meal let the curtain fall. It was the eaters, not the eaten, that had the fascination for me. As it happened, it was only the day before that I had walked through A Street in South Boston. It was vacation, and the wretched Irish children were sitting on their haunches as Baker describes the Abyssinians, looking across the street at nothing with their poor lacklustre eyes. What should they do? Mr. Nash had given them baths. But they could not swim all day! The city had given schools, but they could not go to school all the year! Poor wretches, — afternoon had come, and supper-time had not come, — what room was there in those heated tenements, — what play for them out-doors? And these miserable, pseudo-Abyssinian children were of the same blood as Phelim and Honora and Owen. Nay, maybe they were their cousins. Maybe; — and what is certain, dear reader, is that they were your brothers and sisters, and were mine!

So I drank Mary's tea from her wonderful new service of "chaney." I eat, in the right order, of bread, toast, gingerbread, pie, and tea-cake; I praised the children's berries and had a quart put up for Polly and the children; I kissed the little ones good by, I shook hands with the eldest, cried "All right!" to Phelim as he stopped the horse-car, entered it, crossed to the steam station, and in thirty-seven minutes and nineteen seconds, from house to house, I was at home in Polly's arms.

They did not sell season tickets on the Great Northern; they sold package tickets, and for his six hundred and twenty-four passages yearly Mike had to pay sixty-two dollars and forty cents. His interest money on his house was forty-six dollars and fifty cents. These two amounts made one hundred and eight dollars and ninety cents a year against the three dollars a week which Mike used to pay for two nasty and deadly rooms over the open drain in Back-street-court-place. He had, thrown in beside, the steady improvement in his property, his children's health, the value of their work, as it appeared in the garden and the results of the garden, and, above all, the feeling that no man was his master, that he was independent, was subduing the world, and in short was one of the governing classes. Mike was not the only workman in Naguadavick who saw the advantage of that line of life.

"This is certainly better," I said to myself, as I rode into town, "than having to crowd Mike and Mary and their friends as we did five years ago. All our ministry at large, and all our home missions, and all our provident associations, and all our relief organizations, and all our soup kitchens, were but a poor apology for such a success as this. We are getting back here on the true American principle, 'where every rood of ground supports its man,' woman, and child, — nay, is it not the principle of the prophet: 'Every man shall sit under his own vine and fig-tree'?"

"We must have land enough too," I said. "In a circle of fifteen miles' radius around Naguadavick there are about four hundred and fifty thousand acres. So many acre homesteads, supposing an acre were the average. That gives homes for two million persons, and Naguadavick will not need two million inhabitants, while there are only one million people in the whole State."

And so I returned home.

To live thus, near Boston, and to let our laboring men live thus, we need to provide for the laboring men as carefully as we have already provided for the men who live on salaries. For this, we need express trains from points so distant that land is yet cheap. And we need unswerving regularity in the administration of these trains. These requisites granted, such an arrangement becomes a blessing to Boston, to the neighborhood, to the laborer, and to the railroad or common carrier, who intervenes among them all.

HOW THEY LIVE IN VINELAND.

VINELAND is a village of about three thousand inhabitants, closely surrounded by farms, where there reside nine thousand more, thirty-five miles from Philadelphia, on the way to Cape May.

Eight years ago no person lived in the village thus occupied at the present time, and hardly six families on the lands now used for farms.

No extensive manufacture has called these people together. There has been no discovery of mines, mineral spring, or other marvel. The railroad gives them no new facility, or any which is not shared by a dozen other places. Nor is the soil any better than in a hundred others.

Vineland has become what it is, a busy, thriving place of twelve thousand people, by the steady development of two or three simple principles, which might be tried anywhere, if there were a scale sufficiently large for the experiment.

I contribute to this book, therefore, a brief study of these principles as they have been illustrated by the growth of Vineland. For I believe that in the application of such principles to the settlement of small towns as cities of refuge near our large cities is the salvation of our large cities to be found. I believe these principles are of general application, and that the success of Vineland need be, by no means, exceptional. They are, substantially, the same principles, which, in the sketch here attempted of the life of the people of Naguadavick, are relied upon for the success of the colonies which they established in their railroad villages. As I am well aware, however, that the possibility of founding such villages on these principles will be doubted, I am glad to sustain it by a sketch of the origin and success of Vineland. I ask any person who is incredulous to go and visit that town.

First, and chiefly, Vineland relies, — as the imagined towns of Rosedale and Aboo Goosh rely, — on what I may call the natural passion for holding LAND, and the beneficial effects of FREEHOLD on the Freeholder. We have forgotten these effects in America, simply because land was to be got for the asking in our fathers' days, and is to be got for the asking now in many regions. Therefore, in a social condition formed by men who were almost all freeholders, we neglect the advantages of FREEHOLD as we do those of air, water, light, and the salt sea. But, as we pile people together in cities, — as we separate them from their mother earth, — as we make them tenants of one and another landlord, we do our best to unmake the virtues of two centuries' growth, which sprang from the holding of one's own home in fee-simple. The freeholders of New England, in 1775, were a different

race of beings from the privates in the English regiments under the command of General Gage whom they met in battle. The institutions which they made, when they established, in 1780, the Constitution of Massachusetts, — and when they established afterwards the other constitutions which on that were patterned, — were all based on a supposed state of society, where almost every man owned his home, had a stake in the country, as the English say, and had that steadfast desire to improve the town in which he lived, in all of its institutions, which to such *real* estate belongs. Real estate, indeed! It is the only estate which gives man firm foothold. It represents the only wealth which does not easily take wings and fly away!

So long as the American systems are tested in States where most men still have freehold, as in the State of Vermont, for instance, they work as regularly and as precisely as they ever did. Let me copy literally the opinion of one whose opinion in such a matter is worth much more than mine. I take it from a note on my table addressed to me, which I copy literally, only omitting the name of the town in Illinois where it is written. It is from a boy now seventeen years old, who in Massachusetts knew the inside of at least one jail, and was always in hot water.

"July 27, 1869.

"Mr. Hale Dear Sir i Write these few lines to let you know that i am Well and hope you and your family are the same i have been west onwards two years i have been living on a farm since i came out here i have clothed myself and laid up my money i have been geting $250 a year i have thought of buying a farm and takeing my mother out here if i thought she would come i like this state very well the reason is that a poor man can get a home in a little while if he uses his means proper more so than in the east i wich you would give me some information where my mother is and tell her to write to me as soon as posible as i am anxious about her if you think i am worth noticeing i wich you would write to me as soon as you get this letter and give me some advice on this matter and tell me what you think i had ought to do."

Now that letter is a little deficient in commas, but the spelling speaks sufficiently well for the two or three winters' schools to which this boy was sent in a mountain town in Massachusetts. And I would give more for the letter as an exposition of the real worth of Illinois than I would for fifty "hifalutin" articles in the Chicago or the Springfield newspapers. That Irish boy of seventeen has found the root of this matter. He can get a home in Illinois, though he is poor, and he can send for the half-cracked mother, who spent the best of her life, after her husband deserted them both, in taking care of him.

Land, — or Freehold, — in short, is really a prime necessity. It is necessary that almost every man should have a fair chance at Land, — held in his own right, — if you mean to govern America by its original institutions.

Now if a man means to be a farmer there is no trouble about his getting this land. Between Lord Ashburton's line on the northeast and Cape Florida on the south, and Nootka Sound and the rest of the Pacific Ocean on the west, there is plenty of land — and the best of land, if a man wants literally to subdue the earth — to raise the food from it for his own household, and to sell to the more civilized lands the surplus he has left. According to the free-traders, this is what we all ought to be doing. We ought to stop this singing of songs, wearing of clothes, printing of books, carving of statues, digging in mines, and ought to devote ourselves to the "providential duty" of America in raising breadstuffs and cotton for the rest of the world. But even Adam Smith made books, instead of working at a loom in Glasgow, as by his own theory he should have done. And the good sense of the people of America prefers God's order to the order of the Economists. It prefers to develop each human gift as it appears, and so to vary human industry, that, on our own soil, there shall be fair chance for each class of human power. If Jonathan Edwards happens to be born here, we give him a chance as a metaphysician, though by the theory he should be raising Indian corn. If Allston is born here, we give him a chance as a painter, though he should be raising indi-

go. We once let Eli Whitney try his hand as an inventor, though he should have been laying stone-wall in Connecticut, by the theory. By our latitude in that one case we created the cotton crop of America. We let Fulton build steamboats, and Norris and Ross and Winans build locomotives, and De Witt Clinton build canals, and Nathan Hale build railroads, though by the theory all of them should be hoeing, or at the best grinding. And so, after two or three centuries of varied industry, we have a civilization of the highest grade, — wholly different from the low agricultural civilization of Southern Russia, of Poland, and of Ireland. We have millions of people, gathering in and near large towns for purposes of commerce and manufacture; — and yet we have and we love institutions which are based essentially on the idea that the very great majority of the people of the State shall be freeholders, and shall be controlled, in their motives and in their action, by those considerations which to the possession of Land infallibly belong.

Nobody but Mrs. Partington expects to sweep back these thronging millions from the towns to the prairies by nice little half-column articles in the daily papers, on the joys of Agricultural Life. If the men who write these Idyls like the prairies, why do not they go to them themselves? That is the fierce question which young men from the country and young girls from the country ask, — men and girls who have forced their way to the large towns and their excitements and occupations, precisely because their own tastes or aptitudes lay in the direction of commerce or of handiwork or of fine art, and precisely because they did not choose to continue in the duties which the life of a farmer compelled. We cannot undo the eternal laws of our civilization. We cannot keep our bread and eat it too. We cannot have large cities, with the stimulus they give in civilization, and at the same time send all our young people to fence in prairies, and raise breadstuffs. The plaintive appeals addressed by those who have got their seats for the spectacle to those who are crowding on the outside — that they will all be pleased to go away — are scarcely heard. When they are heard it is by those who are quite incredulous, though they are told that there is not even standing room within.

I. FREEHOLD is taken for granted in the theory of American institutions.

II. COMPACT CITIES are necessary for modern civilization.

How are these two necessities to be reconciled?

Where the cities are not large the tendency and habit of American institutions asserts itself, and the workmen in the shops of cities are at the same time freeholders in the immediate neighborhood of their work. In the city of Worcester, in Massachusetts, there are about thirty-five thousand persons at the present time, of whom I suppose nine tenths are engaged in manufacture. As in all manufacturing towns, the proportion of persons not living in families is large. There were in May, 1868, 9,137 men over eighteen years of age. I suppose five thousand of these may have been heads of families. To live in, these families had 3,849 houses, the average number of inhabitants to a house being as low as eight and nine tenths, — singularly low for a manufacturing town. The number of resident persons, firms, and corporations which pay taxes on real estate was as high as 2,924. It would probably be safe to say that in that manufacturing town one half the voters are freeholders, own their own houses and reside in them, having obtained freehold in the neighborhood of their work. A circle of four miles diameter, of which each point would be within two miles of the city hall, would give twenty-four thousand lots of a quarter-acre each, allowing a quarter of the space for roads and parks. On the usual computation of seven persons to a family, a city whose workshops occupied a square mile might give a freehold of a quarter-acre to one hundred and thirty thousand people, all within a mile and a half of the workshop square; and yet no person should live in a house with more than seven inhabitants.

The advantage which newly formed towns like Worcester have in such regards is very great. In old towns like Boston it is very difficult for the laboring man to get freehold near his work; he becomes a tenant, and the tenement-house system comes in, with all its disadvantages.

But at this point the invention of railroads relieves, or may relieve, the crowd upon the towns.

Any village within fifteen miles of a commercial or manufacturing town is within half an hour of it by express train. Now half an hour between home and work meets the requisition of a laboring man.

A circle of fifteen miles' radius includes rather more than	433.580 acres.
Give a quarter of this, or	108.395 "
to roads and parks, and you have left for workshops and homes.	. 325.185 acres

Give eight thousand acres to shops and warehouses, — that is, a block three miles by four miles in the middle of the circle, — and you have left three hundred and seventeen thousand acres. This, if you chose to divide it so, would be a freehold acre-lot for so many families; for a population, that is to say, of two millions and a quarter, none of whom should live in the " business part of the town," none of them in a house of more than seven inhabitants, and each of them with a garden of an acre.

This is the theoretical combination of the advantages of freehold, and the advantages of compact cities.

But, as every reader knows, the practice does not approach this theory.

1. In cases of seaboard cities a large deduction

must be made for that part of the circle which is covered by water.

2. The railroad companies in general are compassing sea and land to get another barrel of flour or another passenger from a thousand miles away, unconscious that they can make their richer market at their doors. One passenger from New York is shot into Boston with the highest speed science can give, for a thousand who are left to linger along in the doldrums of local trains. But the time of the distant traveller is not a whit more important than that of the neighbor.

3. The landholder thinks his duty done when he cuts his land into small lots and offers it for sale. The truth is that land of itself is the most worthless of commodities. To induce the laborer from the city to buy the land many intermediate steps must be taken. Of many of these steps we have valuable suggestion in the experience of VINELAND.

It is perfectly true that in the neighborhood of all large cities may be seen tracts with the lines of paper roads dimly shadowed on them, with one or two cottages ornées tumbling to ruin, which are held up as the illustrations of the failure of efforts to induce laboring men to live in the country. In truth, they are only illustrations of the folly which supposes that, in a country of intelligent men, any man can sell by the foot at high prices what he bought by the acre at low, without doing anything himself to improve the condition of the property.

1. People will not establish themselves in any village of small holdings, unless it is large enough, or promises to be large enough, to give them society, and, with society, the amusements, the instruction, and mutual advantages of other kinds which society affords. The town must be large enough for two or three churches at least, for good schools, for public entertainments of different grades, and for the vivacity which belongs to city life, or the laboring men will stay in the city. This requires an enterprise involving at least one thousand families. Six hundred acres of land, at the very least, are needed to offer to each settler the attractions which are indispensable. One or two thousand would be better.

In the establishment of VINELAND, Mr. Landis, the founder, was not looking to draw men out from cities. I suppose he would be quite as willing that men used to city life should not come. He was trying to build up a community of small farmers. But even he saw the necessity of compact village life. The centre of Vineland is a village of six hundred acres, crossed by eight streets, running one way, and in the middle of all, by the broad avenue of which the railroad is the middle; — and across the other way by nine streets, with Landis Avenue. The village lots were originally fifty feet wide. Mr. Landis gave land for the erection of churches; and, as he could, encouraged horticultural, scientific, and other societies, which aimed at entertainment and mutual improvement.

Outside of this village, Mr. Landis laid off farm lots, from five to twenty acres and upwards, which now cover a tract of more than forty thousand acres.

I am confident that the success of Vineland is due, first, to the very magnitude of the scale on which it is planned. Most of us would be willing to live in a community of ten thousand people. But it is only exceptional persons who really prefer the solitude of a hamlet of twenty or thirty.

2. The new-fledged freeholder, who has bought himself a half-acre lot in some Mount Vernon or Mount Bellingham speculation near a large city, is apt to find that all the hardships of land-owning come upon him long before the advantages can develop. The day of the auction sale he was quite a hero. He had a free ticket to ride to the spot. He had champagne, crackers, and cheese without charge. He was, that day, the companion and friend of all the directors. The new roads were in perfect order. The trains came and went exactly as the exigencies of the sale required. But, before he has owned his land a month, he has learned that the fence to it will cost him more than the land cost him. The road has washed badly in a shower, and he cannot find anybody whose business it is to repair it. No grocer is yet established in the neighborhood. And the railroad no longer runs a train in and out when it is wanted. He does not know any of the other new land-owners. He finds that the directors of the land company no longer

know him; and that they are naturally quite indifferent to his difficulties. The only new acquaintance he makes is the tax collector, who begins assessing his real estate at the auction price. And when he talks with a mason about building, he is told they must begin by digging a well on each of these little lots, for which he begins to think they have all paid very high.

In Vineland Mr. Landis met most of these difficulties in advance, by methods which, as I believe, must be imitated by any one who wishes for success. He went and lived in his own town, and made the establishment of the town his business. There was at least somebody on hand who wanted to have the establishment succeed. By a master stroke of policy, fortunately easily imitated under the law of Massachusetts, he took away all necessity for fencing, by keeping all cattle closely confined. On the other hand, he bound each purchaser to make certain improvements within twelve months; so that there cannot be in Vineland many of the odious empty corner lots, waiting to become valuable, which disgrace most new towns. Among the improvements required of each purchaser was the seeding with grass of the sides of the highway, the planting of shade-trees along the streets and avenues, and a fixed line was given, before which the fronts of the houses must not be carried. By these arrangements alone many of the drawbacks which sicken a new freeholder of his bargain are effectually removed.

If you go to Vineland, you find near the station a decent-looking hotel, which, when I saw it, made no pretence, but seemed comfortable enough, — which is, clearly enough, in the interest of the proprietor. You enter your name on the book, and, before long, a man accosts you, who asks if you wish to see the place. If you say you do, he says it is his business to show it to you, and that if you like to take his guidance, he will be ready with a carriage when you say, — without charge to you. Meanwhile you can look at the plans, where you will find the prices of unimproved property marked. He will own that he shall try to make you see the place to advantage, that he has a commission on each sale he makes; but you are of course at liberty to go with or without his guidance. Probably you take his guidance. He drives you up and down well-built avenues and roads, shows you village lots, farm lots, the general plan of the settlement, and answers your questions as well as he can.

You finally think you should like such or such a place which you have seen, and say you will go home and ask your wife. "As you please," says the agent, "but if you buy at first hand you must take your chances. If another purchaser appears to-morrow, why, we shall sell to him." If you agree to purchase to-day, favorable terms are given as to times of payment, which extend over four years; but invariably the conditions which have been alluded to are exacted. No person buys, unless he expects to become himself a settler. It is evident, from all conversation with the people of the place, that they have taught themselves to regard any land speculator who comes between the original holder and the inhabitant of the land as an unendurable nuisance. But they do not regard Mr. Landis so, I think. Their purchases have made him rich, and they know it. But he has identified himself with the success of the place. He has kept up the highways at his own charge. The business of the town is raising fruit. Mr. Landis appoints an agent who carries all fruit for the settlers to Philadelphia or New York, sells it, and remits the full proceeds to the producer, without any charge on them. This is, of course, in theory, false political economy. But see at how low a charge it encourages the beginnings of the industry on which the town is to rest. Under a similar policy he has borne the principal part of the expense of draining three hundred acres of swamp, from which muck can be drawn for manure, and has given to each settler the privilege of drawing for his own use as much as he needed. During the winter of 1866–67 fifty thousand wagon-loads of this muck were removed thus by the settlers from the lands of the proprietor for manure for their own farms and gardens. I was told that the settlers went with confidence to Mr. Landis as a friend who would pull industrious men out of difficulties. I see that he is an officer in almost every one of the innumerable societies.

In the year 1866 the Agricultural Society paid an aggregate amount in premiums of two hundred and twelve dollars, while the Floral Society distributed in premiums twenty-three dollars.

In the same year (1866) Mr. Landis distributed the following list of premiums: —

One hundred dollars to be divided in two sums, for the best essay upon the history of the place; to be determined under the supervision of the Historical Society.

One hundred dollars, to be divided in two sums, for the best essay in Prose, and the best in Poetry.

One hundred dollars to the Agricultural and Horticultural Society, to be distributed as premiums for the best specimens in Produce.

One hundred dollars to the Agricultural and Horticultural Society, to be distributed as premiums for the best specimen of Fruit.

One hundred dollars, to be divided into two prize gold medals with proper inscriptions, to the two male and female scholars who shall each be pronounced the most proficient scholar, independent of any other consideration.

One hundred dollars to the two male and female scholars over fourteen years of age, and not over eighteen years of age, who shall each be pronounced the most proficient scholar, independent of any other consideration.

One hundred dollars to the Band of Music, for which they are to give six public concerts, — three in the open air in summer, and three in winter.

One hundred dollars, in two gold medals, with proper inscriptions, to the persons most graceful in and proficient in gymnastics.

Fifty dollars, in a gold medal, to the lady who cultivated the best flower-garden with her own hands.

In addition to the premiums offered by the Agricultural Society in 1867, Mr. Landis offered the following: —

Twenty dollars and certificate for the best acre of broom-corn.

Twenty dollars and certificate for the best acre of field carrots.

Twenty dollars and certificate for the best acre of field turnips.

Twenty dollars for the best kept farm.

Twenty dollars for the best kept orchard, not less than two acres.

Fifty dollars to the lady who cultivates the best flower-garden with her own hands.

One hundred dollars, to be divided between the two male and female scholars, not over eighteen years of age, who shall be pronounced the most proficient scholars.

One hundred dollars, to be divided between the three persons who are the best players on the violin, cornet or bugle, and flute; to be played at the Fair, and decided by the committee.

Fifty dollars to the lady most proficient in gymnastics.

Fifty dollars to the gentleman most proficient in heavy gymnastics.

I may say, in brief, as a summary of this part of my observations on Vineland, that it is the only new place I ever visited where I have found the greater part of the women satisfied. Pioneer life — the establishing of new communities — comes very hard upon the women. The men have the excitement; the women generally have hard work at home without excitement. The men find their society as they do their daily work. The women generally are left alone to theirs. But in Vineland, even when it was but four years old, I found intense activity everywhere, and I spoke to no woman who was not well satisfied with the social experiment which was undertaken there.

3. It will not unfrequently happen that the purchaser fails to make the improvement to which he is pledged, and that the land therefore recurs to Mr. Landis. In this case, when he offers the land again for sale, he changes the price from what it was, as the circumstances may justify. But in general the price of unimproved land remains unchanged, Mr. Landis relying for his profits on the continual improvements of the settlement, which of course quicken sales, as the population enlarges. What reason he has for such reliance may be judged from the following record of progress.

In 1861 one shanty was built on the new village lot.

In 1862 twenty-five houses were built, a store, and a school-house.

In 1863 one hundred and fifteen houses were built, and at the end of the year three hundred and sixty-nine purchases of land had been made.

At the end of 1864 six hundred and seventy farms had been sold; and on the 1st of January, 1865, nearly two thousand persons attended Mr. Landis's annual reception. As a token of regard they presented to him "Appleton's Cyclopædia."

In 1865 about two hundred buildings were erected, and at the end Mr. Landis had sold about fourteen hundred properties. Nearly one thousand contracts to build were made in this year.

At the end of 1867 nearly two thousand farms had been sold.

The following table, recently published, shows what various institutions had come into being in this period. Many of these are doubtless larger on paper than anywhere else, still they represent something.

I. Manufacturing Interests.

1. American Building Block Factory.
2. Twelve Stone Quarries.
3. Three Brick Yards.
4. Six Steam Mills, Planing Mills, and three Lumber Yards.
5. Door, Blind, and Sash Factories.
6. Carriage Factories.
7. Saw and Plane Handle Manufactory.
8. Wood-turning and Scroll-sawing Manufactory.
9. Shoe Factory.
10. Pottery and Stone-Ware Manufactory.
11. Straw-sewing Business.
12. Crates and Fruit-Boxes Business.
13. Bookbinding and Paper-Box and Fancy Varieties Business.
14. Clothing Business.
15. Hoop-Skirt Manufacturing.
16. Button Business.

II. Agricultural and Kindred Societies.

1. Vineland Agricultural and Horticultural Association.
2. Ladies' Floral Society.

[Strawberry Festivals and annual Fair and Exhibition under the auspices of the above.]

3. Pomological Association.
4. Fruit Growers' Association.
5. Co-operative Association.
6. Landis Avenue Improvement Association.
7. East Vineland Agricultural and Pomological Society.
8. South Vineland Fruit-Growers' Club.
9. Lincoln Mutual Benefit Farmers' Club.
10. North Vineland Agricultural and Horticultural Society.
11. Forest Grove Agricultural Society.

III. 'Change and Business Facilities.

1. Private Bank.
2. Safe Deposit Company.
3. Mercantile Association.
4. Vineland Loan and Improvement Association.
5. Three Post-Offices, one of which does a far larger business than any other in West Jersey.

IV. Temperance and Physical Reform.

¶ Intoxicating Liquors Voted out of Vineland, July 10, 1863

§ Township law to that effect.

1. Independent Order of Good Templars.

a. Alpha Temple.

b. Liberty, Excelsior, Rising Sun, and Koh-i-noor Lodges.

2. Health Association.
3. Phil-Athletic Club.
4. Base Club.

V. Educational Privileges.

1. Sixteen District Schools, at convenient distances from all parts of the Tract.
2. Four Private Schools.
3. Classical Institute.

4. Young Ladies' and Gentlemen's Academy.

5. Methodist Conference Seminary, now building, 142 feet long, 56 feet wide at the ends, and 44 feet in the centre. Height from ground to top of cornice, 50 feet. Lofty French roof, spacious cupola, porticos, piazzas, balconies, &c. Style, — Large Italian, (whatever that may be.)

6. Societies of Art and Learning.

a. Vineland Historical and Antiquarian Society.

b. Pioneers' Association.

c. Literary Association.

d. The People's Lyceum.

e. Hamilton Mutual Benefit Society.

f. Vineland Library Association.

g. Harmonic Society, Glee Clubs, and Cornet and other bands, &c.

h. Dramatic Association.

i. Social Science Association.

j. Lectures, exhibitions, festivals, and other varied intellectual entertainments, periodical and extraordinary.

VI. Benevolent Societies, &c.

1. A. F. of A. M.: — Masonic Hall.
2. I. O. of O. F.
3. Philanthropic Loan Association.

VII. Public Halls, Parks, Squares, &c.

1. Plum Street Hall.
2. Mechanics' Hall.
3. Union Hall.
4. The Park, covering forty-eight acres.
5. Thirteen Public Squares.
6. Siloam Cemetery, covering fourteen acres, beautifully laid out.
7. Public Adornments.

VIII. Religious Societies.

1. Episcopalian. — Trinity Church (Gothic), on Elmer Street.
2. Presbyterian. — Church (Light Italian), on Landis Avenue.
3. Methodist. — Church (Romanesque), on Landis Avenue.
4. Baptist. — Reed's Hall. Large Church (Byzantine Romanesque), now being erected on Landis Avenue.
5. Free-Will Baptists.
6. Sabbatarian.
7. Baptist Congregational. — Church (Italesque), in South Vineland.
8. Union. — Church (Italesque), in South Vineland.
9. Adventist.
10. Unitarian. — Church (Plain Gothic,) on Sixth and Elmer Streets.
11. Friends of Progress. — Plum Street Hall.
12. Catholic. — Church soon to be erected.
13. Young People's Union Christian Association.

IX. Miscellaneous.

1. Journalistic.

a. Two weekly newspapers: "Vineland Weekly" and "Vineland Independent."

b. One bi-weekly: "Vineland Democrat."

c. Two monthly: "Vineland Rural" and "Farmers' Friend."

2. Political.

a. Union League.

b. Grand Army of the Republic.

c. Two Campaign Clubs.

The steadiness of the price of unimproved lots is an inducement to every resident to persuade his friends and relatives to come and assist in the enterprise. Almost all settlers, in this way, begin to feel a pecuniary interest in the success of the whole. If a settler and his wife are pleased, — if they see the rapid advance of the value of land, given by some improvement, they become themselves the best advertising agents; they write to relatives or friends to show to them the advantages of an investment here; and thus add to the growth of the establishment. They cannot invest in unimproved lands themselves, without making the required improvements. But they can invite their friends to come and make them, and it is evident, from the rapid growth of the place, that this is what they have done.

That Mr. Landis is himself kindly regarded by the people who have come together in the town which he has founded seems evident from the direction which a thousand straws take, blown by the wind of its popular opinion.

4. Early in the settlement of Vineland the people of the town, led undoubtedly by Mr. Landis, determined, with great unanimity, that they would not have the sale of intoxicating liquor, or what they call "saloons," and we call "bar-rooms." They sent out of town the first dealer who sold beer to the boys and wood-choppers, and called a meeting which passed resolutions, and formed an organization to prevent the sale of intoxicating liquors. This was July 10, 1863.

They then, by a very curious arrangement, petitioned the Legislature of New Jersey, to pass a special law precluding the sale of any intoxicating liquor, beer, or wine, within the limit of Landis township. The

Legislature did this by a vote of sixty-three to four, on the ground, probably, that the people asked for it, as the State of New Jersey has no such general policy. Each offence against this law is punishable by a fine of fifty dollars or by imprisonment or both.

Of course this peculiarity keeps from Vineland all settlers who wish to have the privilege of buying and drinking liquors in public. There is no restriction on a man's buying liquors elsewhere and bringing them to his house to use. But he must not sell them in Vineland. Mr. Landis, and the great majority of the people there, are very willing to give up any settlers whom they thus lose. There is, indeed, in most new enterprises of land-settlement, no lack of openings for them. The result of the policy is shown succinctly in the following report from the Town Constable and Overseer of the Poor, published in the spring of 1869.

As Constable and Overseer of the Poor there are some things in my department which show so conclusively the favorable working of the system upon which Vineland is founded, that I will give the information to the public, so that the facts may be known and the example of this system followed.

The two principles in Vineland which we recognize as uppermost are: First, That land shall not be sold to speculators; second, By the decision of the people that there shall be no grog-shops, liquor saloons, licensed taverns, or lager-beer shops.

What is the practical working of these principles? I will state a few facts which are probably unexampled in the United States, at least. Though we have a population of ten thousand people, for the period of six months no settler or citizen of Vineland has required relief at my hands as Overseer of the Poor. Within seventy days there has been only one case, among what we call the floating population, at the expense of four dollars.

During the entire year there has been only one indictment, and that a trifling case of assault and battery among our colored population.

So few are the fires in Vineland that we have no need of a fire department. There has only been one house burnt down in a year, and two slight fires, which were soon put out.

We practically have no debt, and our taxes are only one per cent on the valuation.

The Police expenses of Vineland amount to seventy-five dollars per year, the sum paid to me, and our poor expenses are a mere trifle.

I ascribe this remarkable state of things, so nearly approaching the Golden Age, to the industry of our people and the absence of King Alcohol.

Let me give you, in contrast to this, the state of things in the town from which I came, in New England. The population of the town was 9,500, a little less than Vineland. It maintained forty liquor-shops. These kept busy a police judge, city marshal, assistant marshal, four night watchmen, six policemen. Fires were almost continual. That small place maintained a paid fire department of four companies, of forty men each, at an expense of three thousand dollars per annum. I belonged to this department for six years, and the fires averaged about one every two weeks, and mostly incendiary. The support of the poor cost two thousand five hundred dollars per annum. The debt of the township was one hundred and twenty thousand dollars. The condition of things in this New England town is as favorable in that country as many other places where liquor is sold.

T. T. CORTIS,

Constable and Overseer of Poor of Landis Township

5. The aim of Mr. Landis, from the beginning, has been to build up a community of which the central business should be small farming. He has no such aims as had the founders of the villages, described in this volume, who wished to make homes for the laborers of Naguadavick. His advertisements, his reports, and his plans all refer to the advantages of the place for light farming, or market gardening or the raising of fruit. To this object he has applied himself, — and in his effort he has succeeded. Of course a great many people are dissatisfied, and go away. In the Vineland papers are long advertisements of improved property offered for sale. But this will happen in all new places. The restless people go to them; the restless people leave them. People who succeed in them leave them for a larger field. People who fail leave them to try other circumstances. Indeed, I think I could show that of a given number of persons in a community, even as settled as is Boston, the chances are, taking the average of years, that one twelfth will have removed from that city before one year is over. Vineland is no Eden or Fairyland. It requires work, perhaps as much as any place in the world. But by a few simple arrangements it is made easy for people with small capital to establish themselves there. It follows that large numbers do establish themselves, and that, of those numbers, a large proportion remains. The following letter from a "comparative cripple" — a carpenter-farmer — will show what has

been done in a single instance, which seems to be in no way exceptional.

VINELAND, Landis Avenue, near Main Road, May 6, 1868.

MR. EDITOR, — I have thought that a truthful record of my farming and "getting along" experience generally in Vineland would be of some importance, especially as bearing on the prospects of success which have hitherto opened, and still continue open here, to an *industrious* person of *small capital.* To that effect I hereby treat you to the following "fireside talk," which can be any day fully verified by the closest investigation.

I have resided in Vineland for four years. I came here with my family, consisting of my wife, one son, who lost an arm at Gettysburg, and two grown-up daughters, from Canaan, Maine. My occupation there was the manufacturing of bedsteads and general teaming, with some little farming. This brought me in, during six years, an average of one hundred dollars clear annually; but I must say that my ambition was but very poorly satisfied with such small "pay" for very heavy work.

As it happened my daughter came across a "Vineland Rural." We all perused it attentively, and, after careful deliberation, unanimously decided that we would give a fair trial to Vineland, more on account of our health than anything else, as we had for some time come to the conclusion that a milder latitude than that of Maine would be decidedly beneficial to us all. And I would here say that I was then a comparative cripple, and have been for a long time constantly suffering from a most annoying chronic disease, which all people, professional and otherwise, naturally pronounced irremediable.

Well, I came and saw Vineland, travelled some over the tract, investigated, thought, pondered, and finally made up my mind to settle. After paying my debts in Maine, and moving my family here, I found that we had left, in all, two horses and one fifty-dollar bill. But we had made up our minds *not* to feel discouraged, come what will. I went at once to work *with my horses*, stump-pulling, at four dollars per day. After a while, and by pretty strict economy, I bought the machine, improved it somewhat, and pulled all the stumps put in my way, " on my own hook." As we had in the mean time (as well as for some time after) no house to go into, I hired two rooms at two dollars per week; bought a small cook-stove and a few other necessary utensils; " kept house in a small way," and got along pretty comfortably on the whole. In a short time, comparatively, I was enabled to pay one fourth cash down, namely, one hundred and twenty-five dollars for twenty-five acres of wild land, five acres on Landis Avenue, on which I reside, and twenty on Chestnut Avenue. Then I bought me another machine, continued to stump for my neighbors and to clear my own land, bought another pair of horses, and also a pair of mules. From then till now, I "kept at it" pretty closely. We all of us lived well enough, got supremely satisfied with the capacities of the soil, raised excellent truck and fruit, and this day I have *all* my land *cleared*, thirteen acres thoroughly stumped, three acres set to grape-vines, three acres in blackberries, two acres in blackcap raspberries, half an acre in Philadelphia raspberries, beside four hundred and twenty-five apple-trees, three hundred and seventy-six pear-trees, twenty peach-trees, with some currant and gooseberry bushes, all in fine growing condition. From what I have tested in the cultivation of sweet and Irish potatoes I have determined to set four acres in each. I also raise every year lots of garden vegetables, — onions, beets, carrots, parsnips, cabbages, &c., — and with this garden produce we are highly satisfied.

My dwelling-house, which I intend to enlarge and trim up generally as we go along, is of wood, sixteen feet by twenty-six main building, with an L thirteen feet by twenty-three, all one story and a half. The stables are thirty-six by twenty-eight. And, by the by, this leads me to state that I intend going into raising grass and hay at no distant day, having already been duly deliberating on *that* subject, as a thing which, by proper attention, will *pay* and *pay well* in Vineland. The nearest calculation I can make, as to what I have done in Vineland, and what Vineland has done to me, is simply this: I know full well, from comparison and the offers which have at times been made to me, that my land and buildings in their present state, show a market value of at least Ten Thousand Dollars ($ 10,000), and that my machines, teams and farming implements are worth at least Two Thousand Dollars ($ 2,000), making up the total of Twelve Thousand Dollars ($ 12,000), which I call my Vineland Industrial Luck. In fact, we would *not* by any means sell out at a much higher figure.

I have never found any place like Vineland for an industrial man to get along in. Besides, it has proven itself, to my experience and knowledge, to be a very healthy place, particularly in my lung diseases. I am myself, for all my hard work, in a much better condition than I had been for long years before moving here. I need not praise our pure, sweet, soft water. The working season, as compared with that of Maine, is just this: you can work out from May to October, or November, at farthest, in that "upper region"; here you can, on a fair average, improve your land from February to Christmas, and sometimes even to New-Year's Day.

My son and daughters have helped me considerably in work; but *they were all well paid.* In fact, except a little during my first summer here, I have had no work whatever done for me which has not been strictly paid for.

My family has not had one single fit of homesickness since we arrived. They are so highly satisfied with Vineland that none of them would leave on any account. Besides, all my children have been well married in Vineland.

There are no two ways about it. A man that has a mind to work, and has some *ambition* in him, will surely get rich, even if partially crippled, and quite as poor as I was when commencing operations here. But if a man will put his little all in a house to begin with, and *will not* keep up his *industry* and *ambition*, why, then he deserves *not* to get rich anywhere, and he has only himself to blame.

Respectfully yours,
CHAS. B. WASHBURNE.

I have said that I know of nothing exceptional in this case. I do not, however, fail to remark, that the name of the writer is that of a family, many of the members of whom, when they have emigrated from Maine, have done so to some purpose, for themselves and for their country.

Here is a most condensed statement, from which I have attempted carefully to prune the enthusiastic declarations which old Vineland settlers always make, of how much they like the place. It is the history of a town, which has been made out of nothing in eight years, without remarkable physical advantages. This town now contains twelve thousand people, living in great comfort, none of whom had large means when they went there. It is a town which evidently is established, and has remarkable prospects in the future. To speak of a single point only, which settlers will appreciate, — here are two hundred miles of well-built roads, in this little tract of say forty thousand acres.

It seems to owe its growth and beauty and prosperity to a few general principles which might be carried out anywhere. In the statement of a Committee at the Paris Exposition of 1867, which gave Mr. Landis a medal as the founder of Vineland, these principles were stated as four.

I. That the land should be laid out with reference to practical convenience.

II. That it should be laid out with reference to beauty.

III. That societies for mutual improvement and entertainment must be formed, and temperance enforced, in order to promote the physical prosperity and mental improvement and happiness of the people. For this, also, small farming and compact population are considered necessary.

IV. The lands and town lots are sold to actual colonists only.

. From these principles spring the details thus described in the same paper by Mr. Landis:—

MATERIAL ELEMENTS.

1. The general plan of laying out the land, by which peculiar facilities were afforded to industrious people to obtain land for homesteads. To accomplish this it was laid out in five, ten, and twenty acre lots and upwards, at a small price, payable in one, two, three, and four years.

2. The requirements that the houses in the town plot be set back from the roadside at least twenty feet, and on the farm lots at least seventy-five feet, in order to afford room for flowers and shrubbery.

3. Requiring all colonists to plant shade-trees upon the roadside, and to grass the roadsides.

4. Requiring colonists to build and settle upon their lands within one year, and selling no land to other than actual colonists.

5. The introduction of fruit-growing and the general improvement of agriculture and horticulture.

6. The introduction of American manufactures.

7. The making of roads and other improvements at my individual expense.

MORAL ELEMENTS.

1. The introduction of good and convenient schools.

2. The formation of agricultural and horticultural societies.

3. The formation of church societies, for the encouragement of morality and religion.

4. The formation of literary societies and libraries.

5. The introduction of a new temperance reform, which, in its practical operation, appears to do away with all the evils of intemperance.

To this statement, which includes the secret of the prosperity of this place, I add the following words from Mr. Landis himself.

"The reason why many settlements fail is because the projectors expect to make an easy speculation of them without much labor and time, and because they have no definite system which will insure the increase of the value of lands upon the hands of the purchasers, as well as the general prosperity of the settlers.

"No prosperous settlement can be made without the personal application by the proprietor of much care and labor over a period of many years. He must expect to make the enterprise an exclusive and legitimate business."

I believe the last statement to embody a most essential suggestion.

Vineland, in short, is a wilderness settlement in the heart of civilization. You have not to carry your family, your furniture, and your stores a week's journey towards the West. You have not to wait a week for your letters from the home you have left behind. I have never forgotten the moment when I first stepped on the platform of the station there. I was in a new settlement, four years only from the wilderness. The people were that day grubbing up the brush where a new church was to stand, in a spot which but just before had been forest. From the car there landed with me two families of the settlers. A woman with one carried a canary-bird. A man of the other waited at the baggage-car for a mould of Philadelphia ice-cream. They were new settlers, — acting like new settlers. But, if they chose, they had canary-birds and ice-cream as well. The incident suggested to me the contrast between Vineland and a log-cabin in township No. 9, in the seventh range.

HOW THEY LIVE IN BOSTON, AND HOW THEY DIE THERE.

"THERE is not one word in the paper," said Laura, as she threw it over to her husband, both of them sitting on the piazza, above the sea at Manchester. "I do not see why they choose to print so much trash from day to day." So she took up Littell's Living Age, and began reading some of Crabb Robinson's *bon-mots.*

For fifteen minutes there was silence.

Bernard laid down the paper in his turn. "I hardly see why you say there is nothing in the paper," said he, looking a little pale and worried. "It is true there is no battle, and there has been no accident on the Erie Railroad for three days; but this account of the death of these poor little children, whose fathers and mothers loved them as much as you and I love Ben, is to me as terrible as a battle, and cuts as near home as a railroad smash."

"Children, — my dear child," said Laura, pale in her turn now. "I saw nothing about children. What is it? Whose children were they?"

Bernard read: —

"From Our Own Correspondent.

"The mortality of the infants in Bethlehem, which has made every Christian mother curse the name of Herod, is more than equalled in the terrible suffering which I do not venture to describe. The *ayuntamiento* appears powerless in the havoc; the physicians give me no encouragement that the plague is stayed. With my companions, I have in the last week attended at the funeral rites of seventy-five of these little innocents; and unless we receive some relief, which we do not anticipate, I shall be obliged often to send to you the same melancholy information."

"Melancholy information!" said Laura, bitterly. "Is the man a stone? — is the agony of a baby and is the wretchedness of the mother only a paragraph in his string of news? Where is this, — in Mexico or in Spain? Why did not I see it? Give me the paper!" And she took it.

"Why, Bernard," she said, after a moment, reproachfully, "you are not making fun of me! You could not make that up to quiz me!"

"No, darling," said Bernard, sadly, looking over her shoulder; "I only added the words for the want of which it missed your eye. There is the story, enough sadder than I made it, and the story will be there next week, and next week, if you take pains to look for it. Only now you know where to look, and you did not know before. The trimming which ladies wear on their summer dresses in Wiesbaden is so important that these people can give a quarter-column to describe that; but the death of seventy-five infants in their own town is only worth half a line of minion. I will make it a little clearer for you. And then with his pencil he drew a line around the words, **CHOLERA INFANTUM, 75,** in the table which I copy below : —

CITY MORTALITY. — The deaths in Boston during the week ending at noon to-day numbered 196, — 102 males, 94 females. Americans, 149 ; Irish, 36 ; English, 3 ; Scotch, 1 ; Provinces, 4 ; Germans, 2. Consumption had 20 victims ; cholera infantum, 75 ; dysentery and marasmus, 11 each ; brain diseases, 9 ; cancer, 5 ; diarrhœa and lung disease, 4 each ; accident, apoplexy, convulsions, intemperance, peritonitis, and rheumatism, 3 each ; diphtheria, debility, infantile and puerperal diseases, typhoid and scarlet fever, old age, premature birth, 2 each ; anæmia, inflammation of bowels, croup, dropsy, fistula, exposure, heart disease, measles, necrosis, paralysis, scald, and syphilis, 1 each. American parentage, 73 ; foreign parentage, 123. — July 31, 1869.

" That means, dearest, that there were seventy-five households fighting death over the cradles of their babies last week, and that seventy-five fathers and seventy-five mothers were defeated, and that life is hardly worth living to them now, because their little ones are not. If it were half round the world, and if it were an *ayuntamiento* that was puzzled, it would make a paragraph ; but seeing it is only in Suffolk Street and B Street, it is not of so much consequence."

" O," said Laura, through her tears, " do not be bitter about it, — these people, as you call them, are no more careless or negligent about them than I am.

We are so happy here and the children are so well," — and she looked anxiously at big, bouncing Ben in his wagon, — "that we forget there are other people in the world. Who are these children? I read the deaths in the papers every day, and there have not been many names of children, — nobody's name that I knew.

"No, dear," said Bernard again, "you did not know them, and I did not, and they are not the kind of people who send their deaths or their marriages to the newspaper. They are the children of the people, who stand up to their knees in water, that the stones may be laid firm that support the causeway on which is laid the gravel that your and my carriage rolls smoothly over. They are the people who, with naked skins in a temperature of a hundred and ten degrees, wheel the coal to the retorts that there may be gas enough at Selwyn's to-night, if you and I fancy we should like to go and see Laura Keene in Midsummer. I do not know," he added after a pause, "how I should have this cigar in my mouth at this moment if there were not a good many of such people somewhere. But, for all that, their names do not get put into the newspapers when they die, unless, by bad luck, somebody kills them."

"Do you mean to tell me," said Laura, rousing herself with something almost of agony in her manner, "that it is sickly in Boston, and that I have not known it all this time? That Emily is there with all her children, in the midst of an epidemic, and that I have not known a word about it? That was not kind!"

"No, dearest," said Bernard again, more sadly than before, — "no, dearest. Emily's children are as safe as yours, probably safer, so far as human wisdom goes. There is no epidemic in Chestnut Street, or Mount Vernon Street, or Beacon Street, or in Worcester Street, or Chester Square, or on Telegraph Hill, or on the Highlands. There is no epidemic anywhere. Only where people live sixteen families in one house, with their swill-barrels in their entries and their water draining on the floors, the chances for life are not as good as they are at Emily's house, where each child has a bath before she goes to bed and a room of its own to sleep in. All I mean is that these people live so that it becomes a very easy matter for their children to die."

Laura sat in silence a few minutes, pushing by Crabb Robinson and the paper both. Then she said to Bernard, "Why is it, Bernard, that I, who have lived all my life in Boston, know nothing about these places that these poor children live and die in?"

"Why is it," said he, "that I know nothing about them, — that I take all I tell you from the printed report of some poor fellow who is trying to thorn up me and the other governors of this country to do something about it? It is simply the old story; as somebody said in London, 'When the nice people of Belgravia and the rest of the West End shall be making their answers at the day of judgment, they will have some reason to say, "When *saw* we thee sick or in prison, and did not minister to thee?"— even after it has been explained to them that seeing one of the least of his brethren is seeing the Lord. For in Belgravia they do not see St. Giles, and as for visiting the prisoners, they would find it hard to get a permit; and as to feeding the hungry, they are afraid to give them potatoes lest they should turn them into beer.'"

"I don't care for that," said Laura, "I do not mean to be cynical or satirical about this thing. I do not live in Belgravia, and there is no place in Boston that I dare not go to, if you go with me. I move we go and see some of the people to-morrow. There is no danger that it would hurt Ben, is there?"

"Not the slightest, child," said Bernard; "we will go as soon as you like. Will you be ready at the 10.28?"

"Yes, or earlier. I will be ready for the early train at 8.40. We will drive up to Beverly and take it there."

So was it that Laura and Bernard made the following observations.

After endless charges to Katy that Ben should be kept out-doors till he took his nap; and that after his nap there should be this and that and the other, they drove to Beverly in time for the early train. It was not more than ten minutes late in Boston; and before ten o'clock they were on their way to the City Hall. Laura felt all the excitement that she felt when she first entered Paris. For, because she had lived in Boston all her life, almost of course, she knew nothing about it. In Paris she had been taken to see the Hotel de Ville, and there was a good deal about it in her journal; in Florence she had, of course, gone to the Uffizzi; in London she had been taken to Guild Hall to see Gog and Magog, but it had never occurred to any one who managed the education of this really well-trained young lady to take her either to the State House in Boston, to see the machinery of the government of the State, nor to the City Hall, to see how that of her native city was carried on. There were pictures at the Uffizzi, and only some photographs at the City Hall.

So there was all the interest of novelty to Laura, as her husband led her up the palatial stairway, and brought her into the City Registrar's handsome office. There was a little of the fear that she was out of her place; but this vanished at once when the Registrar so courteously received her and her husband, though they were both strangers to him. Bernard introduced himself, and said, almost abruptly, being himself perhaps a little nervous, "I am sorry to see you had a bad week last week." The Registrar understood him on the moment, spoke of the seventy-five cholera-infantum deaths, and gave to his visitors such detail as showed to them at once that he was no mere man of figures, and that his tables had to him the terrible interest which Bernard had given to them when he read to Laura. The Registrar stood there and sounded the trumpet week by week, and that with no uncertain sound. If those children died when there was no necessity, his at least was not the responsibility.

He had at once invited Laura into his airy and elegant office, and had given her a chair. In a moment more he brought to her husband the large folio, in which every detail reported to him of the deaths of the last week was written down. Bernard having gained his permission to use these tables, explained to Laura what they were to do.

He had brought with him a little memorandum-book, which he gave to her, that she might copy upon it each of the names of the seventy-five little children who had died from this single disease. She selected these from all the other deaths. She did not enter the birthplaces of the children, nor the names of their fathers and mothers, nor the other facts which she found in the Registry. Her little table, which I will only copy in part, assumed this aspect: —

BOSTON. CHOLERA INFANTUM. July 24 – July 31, 1869.

No. 1. Mary A. Murphy, 1 y. 7 mos., 22 Davenport Street,	Ward	15
" 2. Sarah Eaton, 2 mos., 102 Portland Street,	"	4
" 3. Edith M. Dillman, 5 mos, 19 Trask Place,	"	13
" 4. Gertie F. Tucker, 6 mos., Eutaw Street,	"	1
" 5. John McLaughlin, 8 mos., 61 Prince Street,	"	3
" 6. Mary McCarty, 2 mos., 224 Havre Street,	"	1

and so on.

While she was copying, Bernard, on a little map of the city he had with him, was making red crosses with a pencil, midway in the streets where the deaths occurred. He had finished almost as soon as she had. Then he returned the Registry to the office, with his thanks, and they both went down again to the carriage, leaving for some future day an investigation of the various curiosities of the City Hall.

"Drive to Suffolk Street," said Bernard, as he entered the carriage; and then to his wife, "Well, darling, it begins to look real now. How much more one feels it, when he sees the names of the little things!"

"Do we ever feel anything, Bernard, till we look at it piecemeal, or in the detail? Did you notice, — no, the figures were not on your side of the book, but, Bernard, almost all of these children are less than a year old. Now we always thought that the second year, while they were teething, was the dangerous year for children. But see there," and she took out her note-book, "in my first twenty-two names there is Will Sullivan, three years old; one boy of one year, and one girl of one year and seven months, and all the others are less than a year." She found afterwards that on her whole register there were but eight who had passed twelve months.

"Now," said Bernard, "look at my little map." And he showed her the map. "The worst street," said he, "is Island Street, down on the flats in Roxbury, where the bad smells come from. If you had ever been there you would wonder that any of them were left alive. But of old Boston, which is all we can do to-day, here are the places."

"Queer," said Laura; "they are in two rows, with a white belt, half a mile wide between."

"Yes; but that belt, you see, is the business part of the town, where nobody lives, and Fort Hill, which they are digging down, and it is the Common and Beacon Hill. Here at the North End is Copp's Hill; you see nobody has died there. On the original three mountains of Boston, on its high lands, not one of our seventy-five babies lived or died."

Laura studied the list then with some care. There was not one child on her list from Beacon Street, Chestnut Street, or Pinckney Street. And it was not merely hillsides that were exempt. There were no deaths in Union Park, Worcester Street, Springfield Street, Chester Square; not one death in any of the very nice streets where most of her friends lived and she visited most. And the largest parts, as she had said, were in two clumps together.

"What are these clumps?" said she.

"This on the north is what used to be called the Millpond. It was filled up half a century ago. Of the thirty-seven children whose homes I could find, seven lived there.

"This on the south is the Church Street district, joined to the region north of Dover Street. They are trying now to raise the Church Street district. In this clump there are fifteen children.

"This death in Eliot Street must have been on upland; these in Russell Place and Phillips Place, and these in Prince Street, Cooper Street, Holden Court, Langdon Place, and Samoset Place, at the North End. But of all the other thirty, I think the homes were where God Almighty made the water flow. But it is not that so much. It is that the poor wretches have no air. What was it Sargent used to tell us, that the science of health was the science of getting people into pure air. You shall see as soon as we set foot on the ground what chance there is for breathing, night or day. They have fared well enough in Rutland Street, Waltham Street, Tremont Street, on Commonwealth Avenue, Newbury Street, and Marlborough Street, though these streets are all on made land. These are well-drained and well-aired streets. Air is what you want. Now look here."

The carriage stopped at the corner of Dover and Suffolk Streets, and the coachman asked, "What number?" But Bernard dismissed him, telling Laura that for what was left they had better go on foot. So they came to a wooden house, with rooms each side of the door, two stories high with attics; not so large, as he bade her observe, as the house they had left in Manchester.

"How in the world are you going to get in?" said Laura, timidly.

"O, I shall walk in," said Bernard, and he did, the door being wide open. He tapped at the first door, and immediately a stout Irishwoman appeared, to whom Bernard addressed himself. The moment there was any evidence of conversation, she was joined by another and another.

Bernard whipped out a little note-book and pencil.

"Can you tell me, ma'am, how many families there are on this floor?"

"There 's four, sir, live in here, and this woman lives in the room opposite."

"And how many children are there?"

"I 've got one girl, and Mrs. McDaniel here, she has two boys, and Mrs. McEna she has one girl and two boys, and Mrs. Liener here, she has one boy," and Mrs. Liener blushed and was pleased and confirmed the statement. Bernard asked if they had all been vaccinated, and was assured they had, with the additional assurance that the McDaniel boys were men grown. Meanwhile Laura availed herself of the freedom of a free country to look into the rooms right and left of her which the interlocutors had left open that they might enjoy the colloquy.

Up stairs then proceeded Bernard, Laura following. The first door gave no answer to his tap, the second was wide open, and Laura saw a woman lying on the bed, not asleep, however. Laura took the census here, — there was this woman, who had two boys, Mrs. O'Brien, who had one girl, and Jerry Regan, who had no children, who occupied the four rooms on this floor. Up stairs in the attics were only the McDonalds (other McDonalds from the first floor), and the Farnums, each with one boy. Here were nine families, but none of them were named K*****.

So Bernard asked the second Mrs. McDonald if there were not a little child named K***** who died here last week.

"O, that, sir, was in the basement," said Mrs. McDonald. And it proved that they had let the basement go by, not suspecting that there was any.

Thus far the twelve rooms, of which they had inspected eight, were almost exactly alike, but that four were attics. Rooms nearly square and about ten feet by twelve. Some of them had two bedsteads in, always with high cumbrous head and foot boards, while in one, as Laura observed, which had a cooking-stove, there was no bedstead. Some of them were tolerably neat, — one, in which the woman was lying down, hopelessly dirty. Of the children spoken of, they had only seen one. He was the junior McDonald, in the attic, who, under the auspices of Mrs. McDonald and Mrs. Farnum, was walking his first steps, and crowed and laughed at the visitors very prettily. All the other children had sought wider quarters. From this inspection they went down the narrow stairways, into what was called the basement. It was almost wholly below the street, and in no way differed from what is usually called a cellar. Here they found Mr. Kellarin and Mrs. West, but still no Mrs. K*****. The floor of the entry was wet from the overrunning of the water-faucet which supplied the house, and all the region was damp, as a cellar is apt to be which is much below the tide level. Bernard asked Mr. Kellarin, who seemed to be rather cross, if Mrs. K***** did not live here. "No, — no such woman here!"

"But did not a little child die here last week?"

"O yes, — that was in the back room; no one is there now. She has moved next door."

"Thank God for that," said Laura to her husband, as they crossed the wretched alley. "Nothing can be worse than where she was."

True enough. That floor was wet from the slop of the water. The air was wet, because the sun never kissed it. The rooms were so chilly and so dark! And the smell!

Across the alley was a little brown house about as big as the coachman's house at Manchester. It was every way nicer than that they had left, though so small. Here poor Mrs. K***** came to meet them at the first door. Laura felt that it was she, she looked so sad and so sick. Just a black rag of some kind she had put around her, and when Laura spoke to her kindly and asked about her little boy, and the poor woman told her it was her only child, and that he was sick such a little while, the two women were sisters. The four families in this house were all young. K*****, Leonard, Driscoll, Agin, with their wives, — they all had but two boys and one girl, — only seven people to live in four rooms, which if you had put them together would have made one of twenty feet square.

In the house opposite, which they had visited first, were thirty-one persons in fourteen so-called rooms. What had been the yard of this house had been taken up by another tenement building.

I must not attempt to tell in such detail of each of the visits which Laura made this busy morning. Bernard told her, as they drove back to the train at ten o'clock, that she had knocked off more calls in her three hours than he ever did in his most successful work of his most successful New-Year's Day of his bachelor life in New York. "You have added to your visiting list," said he, "as nearly as I can make it up at this moment, thirteen Mrs. Flahertys and twelve gentlemen of that name, — eleven Mrs. Sullivans, — six Mrs. Feenans, and their husbands, — three Mrs. McLanes and two Mrs. McTanes, — besides miscellaneous names not to be mentioned."

"Well," replied Laura, stoutly, "I wish all my other friends were as cordial to me as these good women have been, — I wish they would be half as well employed when I called on them, — and I wish, on the whole, that they made as much of their advantages as these people do of what we cannot call their advantages."

It is certainly true, that in many instances the instinctive vigor of a woman, and that Divine Principle which has given to a wife the establishment and the comfort of a home, — which among this class of persons is a principle still respected and accepted, — sustain the women who are forced to live in these crowded cells with their husbands and children, so that they often retain decency, order, and even neatness, where one would say it is impossible. Sweetness of air, freshness, or cheerfulness, it is, of course, wholly beyond their power to give.

Laura and Bernard had been snubbed scarcely anywhere. Once, when Laura was the spokeswoman, and asked, timidly, "Does not Mrs. Weiss live here?" she got a very sharp "No." When poor Laura varied her question, the answer was, "No, she died here"; and Laura, who had only taken note of children's death on her memorandum-book, found that mother and child had died together. The landlady, to whom she was talking, knew nothing of her tenants, — or pretended to know nothing, — and made haste to usher her guests out of the wretched grocer-shop, where, if they had asked for bad whiskey, they would have had good chance for more cordial welcome.

They called at one house which always reminds me, as I go to my train, of the front of a menagerie cage, where the little monkeys may be seen among a few of larger growth, performing behind. It is four stories high, and has no entry or hall in it, every room opening by its one door on the four front piazzas which rise above each other. Each room has, in the rear, two closets only lighted from the doors, one of which may be eight feet square; the other is narrower. The front room, which opens on the piazza, is fifteen by thirteen perhaps. This is a suite for a family. And any day you pass you may see the children of forty such families disporting themselves on the piazzas. The reason why there are no windows in the back wall is that there is another similar building, which has been squeezed in there in a space so narrow that it is not nine feet from the windows and doors to the wall opposite, — and, of that nine feet, four or five must be given to the piazza. Stop on your way down Lincoln Street, Mr. Alderman, and look at that building; do not be satisfied with the Lincoln Street front, but try the other front, and guess what are the chances for life there. As the building is arranged, it will "accommodate," I believe, sixty families, — nearly as many human beings as would be permitted by the United States statute on an emigrant vessel of the same size. Yet on the emigrant vessel there are windsails to pump out the air, — there is the certainty of fresh air on deck, and the best of it. And there, at the worst, the imprisonment is but for a few weeks. But, in this anchored hell, the child who is born must live five years before he has wit enough and strength enough to run away.

Here are Bernard's notes on the houses where he

and his wife first called. I have only described the first tenement of the first two.

13 EMERALD STREET. Two tenement-houses adjoining each other. There are thirteen families in one and ten in the other. The water-pipes are put up in the most shameful manner. They must of necessity freeze up at the very first frost. Only one faucet for each tenement-house, — i. e. twenty-three families have two faucets to draw from. There is no way of getting to the faucet without wading in dirty water, the drains being all out of order. Two of the most filthy privies entirely open for these twenty-three families, — so much out of repair as to be dangerous to enter. The boards are broken away, so that you can see into the vaults. The only reason why the people in the houses are not all dead is because they keep their own places much cleaner than anybody could naturally expect. Miserable places, out of repair, the plastering off the walls and ceilings, — no chance to whitewash, for there is no place to whitewash in many of the rooms.

TENEMENT-HOUSE 73 MIDDLESEX STREET. Sixteen families live in this house. The staircase is so narrow and dark that it is a wonder how the children, with whom it abounds, are not daily injured. In the event of a fire it might be that not one of the families up stairs could be saved. There is very fair accommodation here for water. No water-closets, however, and but one privy in four compartments for the whole sixteen families. The passages below are in a filthy condition, owing to unsuitable arrangements for the refuse.

Their whole inspection was on the southern side of the white stripe across Bernard's map. And they had not time that day to go to Island Street. Once or twice they came upon nice, cheerful houses, where Laura said the people had good friends, she was sure, and she would not offer her sympathy. But there were many of these poor Irishwomen who were glad of her visit, and with whom she will keep up her visiting acquaintance long.

"I know," said Laura, as they rode home, "that you hate to be constantly making laws, and controlling people by laws, and I know how your father says that the best government is that which governs least; but I should think something might be done to give such people as these a better chance."

"My dear," said Bernard, "our system in Massachusetts about laws is that of Ensign Stebbins. We take great pains about making the laws, and we take equal pains to let them alone when we have made them." And Bernard took from his pocket a little blue pamphlet which contained the tenement law of 1868.

"How many of these houses had a fire-escape? Did you notice?" said he.

"What is a fire-escape?" replied Laura. "Did any of them have one?"

"Not that I saw," said Bernard. "But here is the act: 'Every such house shall have a fire-escape.' That is Section 3. From Section 4 I learn that these water-closets in Emerald and Middlesex Streets must have been 'approved by the Board of Health.' From Section 6 that that basement in Emerald Street could not have been occupied 'without a permit from the Board of Health'; nor at all unless it was 'perfectly drained.' From Section 8 I learn that all these houses must 'have suitable conveniences for garbage,' and so on, and so on.

"How many times have you noticed the owners' names to-day?"

"Not once," stared Laura.

"Nor I. But listen: 'Every tenement or lodging house shall have legibly posted or painted on the wall or door in the entry the name and address of the owner,' — that is the law, dear Portia. And here is the law about whitewash: 'Every house thus occupied shall be whitewashed every April and October.' My dear, the law might have been made for Sybaris. But the only time I ever heard of a prosecution under it, an ex-mayor defended the landlord, knew how to rip up the indictment, and that was the end of that. O, there is law enough, dear child."

"Well, what can we do?" persisted Laura.

"Do, child? We can make public opinion. The first time Dr. Shurtleff asks you to go to ride, ask him to stop and call with you on some friends of yours in the Crystal Palace. That is the best thing you can do."

But, for himself, Bernard sent me his observations, and I determined to print them.

I CONFESS that I was surprised, when I first looked over this list of seventy-five deaths by cholera infantum in the last week of July, to see that, of the whole number, twelve were in the three wards which are made of the territory of Roxbury. It seemed curious, at first sight, that the mortality in a so-called country town, just now annexed to the compact city, should be even larger in proportion to the population than that of the more compact section. But a moment's examination of the localities removed my surprise. These eleven deaths were all of them in houses on the low, flat land, which would once have been called salt-marsh, which ought, perhaps, never to have been built upon at all, without such elevation of the streets as should give proper drainage to the houses. All of them but two or three proved, on inquiry, to be in tenement-houses of the most crowded character.

My first visit among them was in Island Street; it is not yet accepted by the city, which takes no responsibility for its drainage or its grading. It will be known by residents in Boston as the street which leads to the so-called "Island," where were the odious bone-burning establishments. Here twin children had died in a hut, standing by itself, worth its annual rental perhaps, which I think would be considered in any comfortable country town in New England unfit for the residence of men, but which here was regarded by its occupants as particularly desirable because they were alone. Two of the other deaths were in Adams Street and Chadwick Street, which, though they run down upon the flats, are occupied by a class of tenements much superior to the others. I visited every tenement in Phœnix

Place, which is a fair enough illustration, in its melancholy uniformity, of the whole class. It is a narrow court of eight houses, — four on each side. They are lightly built of wood, all on the same plan. The two end houses have each a shop in one side. All the houses are parted in the middle by an entry with a staircase; — on each side of this entry is a "suite" of rooms, always two. In no case did I find any family occupying more than these two rooms. Deducting the shops, then, here were thirty tenements, — each of two rooms, — and these were occupied by thirty families, of which the smallest was a man and his wife, — the largest a man and his wife with eight children. The population was sixty adults and sixty-five children in the sixty rooms, each of which was perhaps twelve feet square. The summer atmosphere of these places is odious, but I believe it is better than the winter atmosphere. The houses have the great advantage of standing separately from each other, so as to admit of end windows, and ventilation between every series of four tenements. But the lots are so small that all privy arrangements and deposits of offal are horribly near the open windows. The wretched way in which a woman in such a house tells you that her baby died yesterday, as if the child died of course, and she never ought to have expected that it would live, is a sad enough intimation that the tenants themselves know the risk they are running.

I have not cared to go into detail, however. My

object is accomplished in calling attention to the single fact that of these eleven deaths in Roxbury, by cholera infantum, not one took place on the proper upland. In the mortality of the same week in the peninsula of old Boston, out of thirty-eight such deaths, none took place on either of the hills, and only eight on land which had never been flowed over by the sea.

In the epidemic among children in the summer of 1864 one thousand children of less than five years of age died in Boston in one hundred days. I suppose that of the Boston people who read these pages not one in ten knows that there was any such epidemic. It did not rage among the children of people who read Fields and Osgood's books; it raged in such places as I have been describing.

If the deaths had been proportional among all classes of society, at least ten of these deaths would have taken away infants from the parish of which I am a minister, which embraces about one per cent of the population of the city.

But that is a body of people in comfortable circumstances, living in comfortable homes. And, in fact, in that epidemic not one of our children died. So untrue is that

"Pallida mors æquo pulsat pede pauperum tabernas regumque turres." *

* "Pale death steps on with equal step; although
A hut or palace is the scene of woe."

HOMES FOR BOSTON LABORERS.

IN addition to the statement I have made, as to the houses in which the greater part of the laboring men of Boston live with their families at the present moment, I am tempted to add some facts as to the details of the arrangements which might be made for them. They might all own their own houses, — as so many of the laboring men do in our smaller cities, — and yet, at the same time, follow up their daily work in the very heart of Boston. To illustrate this possibility, I have published here the ideal sketch of the life of the suburbs of Naguadavick. To show some of the detail in practice, I have published the historical sketch of Vineland and its neighborhood. The object of this volume is not fulfilled, unless it shows how similar arrangements may be carried out for the laboring men of Boston.

I know very well that many persons suppose that such arrangements are made thoroughly well now. They know that there are a great many pretty villages around Boston, from which crowded special trains run in every morning, and to which they return at night. And people who will read this book will be apt to say that anybody who wants to live in Melrose or Newton or Hyde Park now can do so; that there needs no urging either of capitalist or of laborer; that the residence of laboring men in the suburbs is a thing which will settle itself, and may be left to settle itself.

I am to reply, then, to this comfortable *laissez faire* notion first of all. I have to say, that, as matter of fact, it is not true that what we call, popularly, the laboring men and women of Boston live in any considerable numbers in the suburbs reached by railway. Many of them live in Charlestown, Roxbury, and South Boston, where they can use the short lines of street cars to go to their morning work. But this number, even, is inconsiderable, compared with the large number of day-laborers needed for the day's work of the city. Of the classes of skilled workmen, of whom we do not speak as day-laborers, a considerable proportion live in the suburbs accessible by steam, — the places where they can obtain freehold. Mechanics, clerks in retail or wholesale stores, bankers' clerks, and other persons whose incomes are a little above the wages of the day-laborer, so called, avail themselves freely of the relief which even in their present management the steam railroads give, and bring up their children thus, — where only, perhaps, children should be brought up, — in the country. But the number even of these who are thus provided for is much smaller than could be wished; and the arrangements in many regards are cumbrous and inconvenient. Granting, however, that they can take care of themselves, there is left the much larger class of women who work in shops or stores, and the class, yet larger, of men who work as porters, or stevedores, or as hod-carriers, or at other hard labor in building or in factories, — who live, as they suppose from necessity, in such hired tenements as have been described. They no more think of the possibility of their purchasing their own homes than they think of translating the Hebrew Bible. Of one hundred and thirty sewing-women engaged at Jordan and Marsh's sewing-rooms, September 7, 1869, ninety-three lived in Boston proper, twenty-three in South Boston and East Boston, and only fourteen out of town. Of eighty-two the same day at work at Hovey & Co.'s, forty-five lived in Boston proper, twenty-seven in South Boston and East Boston, and only ten out of town.

I have to say, next, that emigration, though it be only emigration for ten miles, has, in fact, never thriven in this world, unless it has been well led. Unless, at one or another period of the emigration, the way has been smoothed and prepared by men of intelligence, and by the union of the several interests engaged, no emigration has ever gone forward prosperously. The people of this country are utterly indifferent to what they owe to the men who contrived the magnificent system of the Land Laws of the United States, which of themselves give exactly the encouragement to the

Western emigrant that I would secure for the emigrant whom I would lead from Lucas Street into Dorchester to-day. And, for an instance on the other side, the reason that the South, eager for emigration to-day, cannot lure the laboring men it needs into its waste fields by all its magnificent promises, is because no set of men care enough for that wave of civilization to put themselves humanely and deliberately at work, on a large scale, for the organization of emigration southward.

In the old communities of Greece this thing was better understood. To lead a colony, and thus to establish a state, was considered by Miltiades, and Themistocles, and Alcibiades, and Lysias, and Isocrates, — not to name a hundred others, — as being an honor as great as man could claim. I wish there were more of such ambition among the young men of spirit, of fortune, or of education, whom I meet every day, wondering and even asking what America has for them to do, now that the war is over. I remember that Lord Bacon classed the founders of cities among the first of men.

As the people of Naguadavick found, — in the experience of their history contained in this volume, — the enterprise of establishing a "suburb of ease" for laboring men near a great city requires the co-operation of three sets of people, who are wholly unused to act together. It requires the co-operation of the owner of land, of the managers of the railway, and of the settlers who are to buy their homes. Neither of these will move, if he have not confidence in the other.

1. The owner of the land must be willing to devote from six hundred to a thousand acres within half an hour's ride by steam of the city to the enterprise. He must look for sure but not exorbitant profits, to be secured within ten years.

2. The railroad managers must look to the growing up of traffic where at beginning there is absolutely nothing; and, because that traffic is to be all their own, they must at the outset provide for it much more accommodation than its present returns will warrant. It is at this point, as I believe, that most such plans break down. The companies are willing to sell their tickets cheap enough, but they are not willing to run their trains at the outset often enough or fast enough. They want the village to exist before they grant the trains. But nobody will go to the village until they grant the trains.

3. No one laboring man will bell the cat in such an enterprise. No one will go alone, — nor will ten families go alone. The provisions must be generous enough to induce at once general attention among large numbers of people, or they will none of them move. The reasons for their hesitation are obvious.

I am glad to believe that at the present time there are good reasons for expecting the frank and generous co-operation of all these classes in the neighborhood of Boston, upon the true principles which may insure success. The questions connected with such emigration have been discussed more than any others at the meetings of the Suffolk Union for Christian Work. They never came up for discussion there, but some intelligent man, who had watched the present difficulties, brought forward some important contribution towards their solution. The lines of railway running from Boston are so many, and pass through country so favorable for the purposes proposed, that every thoughtful traveller sees the possibility of relieving the city by colonies in its neighborhood. Fortunately these railways are in the management of men who, in general, understand that their interests and the interests of the public are identical in these matters. And the present condition of the worst tenement-houses in Boston is such as to compel the attention of laboring men and their families to any well-considered arrangements for their relief. Indeed, if the trade and manufacture of Boston are to enlarge in the next twenty years in the same proportion as in the last twenty, some systematic provision of healthy homes for her laboring men and women is the very first necessity of all.

I have attempted in this volume to show that that provision may be made by a system which shall involve the following details: —

I. A village site of say a thousand acres.

II. This must be generously laid out by the proprietors, who must maintain on the spot active agents, to care for the proper condition of the town till it can go alone.

1. These agents must keep the roads in condition.

2. They must see that drainage is systematically cared for.

3. In some localities it may be necessary that the first owners sink the wells.

4. All negotiations with the railroads must, at the outset, be made by the first owners.

III. The land should be divided, for our purpose near Boston, into lots of about 10,000, 20,000, and 40,000 feet, to provide for settlers of various resources. These lots should be offered for sale on easy terms, with great encouragement, however, for cash payments. Mr. Landis requires one fourth down, and the remainder in three payments in three successive years. The Illinois railroads require one tenth down, and the remainder in nine payments in nine successive years. Probably the first arrangement is the better for our purpose here.

The price of lots having been fixed at the outset, so as to give a handsome profit to the original landholder, should never be changed by him.

All sales should be made on condition of considerable improvements to be made within twelve months. This is necessary to assure the first settlers of neighbors and society, and to prevent land speculation.

IV. The co-operation of the original holders with

the settlers in all enterprises of social improvement, education, and amusement must be heartily and intelligently granted.

V. The railroad companies, looking to the steady growth of such a village, must provide from the first, *and must assure*, trains of cars which will place the laboring man at his work in Boston at seven in summer and at eight in winter.

It has been proposed by Mr. Quincy, who has taken so cordial an interest in such plans, that most of these companies, for the foundation of a new village in the view here advocated, shall give a free ticket for five years to each head of a family who will build a house in such a town. Then rely on the travel of the members of his family, and of other persons, for their profit. This seems to me honorable, simple, and satisfactory. I should ask nothing more in addition but careful study of the hours of trains required by laboring men, and some security for their permanence.

As to the methods by which such men are to get the money with which to build their houses, I will add a few words; but I do not believe the difficulty in the business will be found there.

Mr. Quincy has published in the daily journals details of the co-operative house-building systems of Philadelphia and of England, which have worked so satisfactorily that I need only refer readers who are interested to them.*

* See, for one of such plans, Appendix A.

I am assured that at Hyde Park, near Boston, the public offer is made by responsible parties, that they will lend to any person who proposes to build there three thousand dollars for that purpose, if he invest, beside, three hundred dollars of his own, and pledge the whole to them. They are so confident of the increase of the value of real property in that town, that they are ready to lend on mortgage of real estate, with so small a margin, at the present time. This is an illustration of the facilities offered in such places.

In the German savings-banks there is a system which carries out with great simplicity the co-operative idea. The managers of those banks discount regularly to their depositors, on a regulation universally understood. It is this: any depositor who can get two fellow-depositors to indorse for him can obtain a discount from the savings-bank, which thus becomes, not a bank of deposit for small sums only, but a bank of discount for small sums. In the town of Worcester, to which I have already alluded in these pages, its prosperity is largely due to the readiness with which the capitalists of the town have assisted the young mechanics and laborers in establishing themselves. It is this readiness to give credit on fair terms which has done so much to make that a place of FREEHOLD.

The details of the German system are given by Mr. Godkin in his valuable paper published in the North American Review two years ago.

I apprehend, therefore, that working men and working women will have no real difficulty in building houses for themselves or in buying houses ready built, so soon as the places are arranged where these houses shall stand. The social condition might return of the agricultural New-England town of two generations ago, in which a rented house was an exception to the general rule and habit of the community. The large rents which laboring men are now accustomed to pay have trained their families in habits of economy which will make it very easy for them to obtain dwellings of their own, as soon as these dwellings are offered to them. For the cells which have been described on page 171 the weekly rent is two dollars for one room and the two dark closets adjoining. This is about the lowest rent which any laboring man with a family pays for a home in Boston. Most of them pay more. It is easy to see how fast an annual payment of only one hundred and four dollars a year will eat up the principal and the interest of such a home as such a man may build for himself the moment land is offered him at a fair price. And the passion for Freehold is not extinguished among these people by a generation or more of tenant life. It is pleasant to conceive the ready response they would make to a programme like this, put in their way in the columns of their friends, the Boston Herald or Boston Pilot, handed into their doors on a broadside, or posted at the street corners.

BUY YOURSELF A HOME!

One Hundred neat Houses are for sale in the new Village of

MONTGOMERY,

ONLY TWENTY MINUTES' RIDE FROM BOSTON!

By a weekly payment of

ONLY THREE DOLLARS,

any man may own, in six years' time, a pretty House and a Garden

RENT FREE!

☞ Large deductions can be made to purchasers who have cash in hand.

Free Railroad Ticket for Five Years!

An announcement like this would show very soon that the laboring class of people are not without reserved funds to draw upon, if they have only a simple and safe way to place them in real estate for their own uses.

APPENDIX.

APPENDIX.

A.

THE Constitution of a Co-operative Society for Building, which has worked well in Philadelphia, is explained in the following letters from Mr. Quincy and Mr. Davis.

MODERATE HOUSES FOR MODERATE MEANS.

I would now call your attention to a communication sent to me by Edward M. Davis, of Philadelphia, describing the workings of an association of which he is president, calculated to aid the frugal and industrious in *securing homes now* payable *out of future earnings:* —

It is *called* a Building Association, but *should* be called a "Co-operative Deposit and Loan Company," as it does not have homes built, but does receive and loan money.

There are 74 members and 1,000 shares. None of the officers receive pay, except the secretary, and he only $ 2 a month. The treasurer gives bonds for $ 1,000, but seldom has over $ 50 to $ 100 on hand, as the money is generally loaned the same night it is paid in to the association. We meet in a school-house and have no rent to pay. Fuel and a janitor costs us about $ 15 a year. It is conducted for the benefit of the members, and not for the benefit of the officers, as is the case with many loan associations.

The receipts of the association are: —

1st. "Dues" of members, consisting of fifty cents a share, payable monthly.

2d. *Fines* of five cents a share each month as penalty for failure to pay punctually.

3d. *Premiums* on money loaned paid by members who borrow.

4th. *Interest* received monthly at the rate of six per cent per annum on money loaned. When from these sources the shares are worth $ 100 each, a distribution is made in the proportion in which the stock is held, and the association comes to an end.

Only members can borrow money. Each one can borrow $ 100 for each and every share, but not over $ 1,500 at one time. The borrower must give to the association as security a first mortgage on real estate for the amount borrowed, and if there are buildings, they must be insured and the policy transferred to the association. The borrower must also transfer the stock on which he borrows; must pay the premium cash; pay his dues and interest punctually, and all expenses of conveyancing.

Our association was started twenty-two months since. As fifty cents each month has been paid on each share, the amount *paid in* is $ 11, but the shares are worth $ 14.10; the difference has been made out of premium, interest, and fines. Judging from the operations of other similar associations, by the time $ 60 has been paid in by members as "monthly dues," the shares will be worth $ 100 each; that is, the association will hold claims on the real estate of the members, and cash on hand, amounting to $ 100,000.

The loans are made by the president, stating that there are say $ 500 in the treasury, but that he will sell $ 1,500 if it is wanted, payable out of the first money in the treasury. Some one is willing to pay five per cent premium for it, another eight per cent, others more, and so on until it reaches say twenty per cent. The buyer has fifteen shares, and says he will take the $ 1,500. He gives security for $ 1,500, and pays interest monthly on the $ 1,500, but the premium of $ 300 is deducted and he gets only $ 1,200 in money. His monthly dues are $ 7.50 and his interest $ 7.50. He therefore pays $ 15 a month until the shares are worth on the books $ 100; then his mortgage is handed back, marked paid, his policy retransferred, and his home is clear. This occurs at the same time necessarily with every borrower, for it is not regulated by what he pays for his money, or when he gets it, but by the *period when the shares amount to* $ 100. When they do all the borrowers are out of debt. If there is cash on hand it belongs to those who have not borrowed, and will be just $ 100 a share for them.

The time that it takes for a society to "run out," as it is called, depends mainly on the *premiums paid.* If they are low the period is over ten years. If they could *average* twenty per cent the period would be much shorter. Money borrowed in the first year of the association at twenty-five per cent premium does not cost the borrower quite eight per cent per annum. Then he has these great advantages; he can borrow an amount almost equal to the cost of his property; can return it in small sums, and in addition participate in the profits made by the association. It is the true mode of getting a home out of *future earnings.* Being the prospective owner of the place occupied, all the improvements inure to him. This system makes our small houses more tastily and insures their being kept in better order, because a home that is *owned* is more cared for than one that is rented. I think that what are called building associations contribute much more towards securing homes to our mechanics and laboring people than our ground-rent system.

A person paying $ 15 a month by this system at the end of about ten years has his house clear, but if he pays the $ 15 as rent, at the end of the ten years the landlord has the rent and the *house too.*

To carry out a plan like this it is necessary at first that some philanthropic persons in whom the people have confidence should, like Mr. Davis, be willing gratuitously to devote a few hours every month to the management of such an organization. As in the case of savings-banks, the success of one might lead to results in the highest degree beneficial both to the public and individuals.

JOSIAH QUINCY.

B.

LAW FOR REGULATION OF TENEMENT-HOUSES.

When the sketch of Life in Boston was published in the Boston Advertiser, I was sorry to find that some of the readers supposed the allusion to the Tenement Law was ironical; and that I only suggested what law there should be.

Our Tenement Law is very well drawn up, based on the Law of the State of New York, which was suggested by the experience of the Board of Health of the city of New York. In the hope that it may be of use to persons interested in this subject in other cities, I copy it in full here.

[CHAP. 281.]

AN ACT *for the regulation of Tenement and Lodging Houses in the City of Boston.*

Be it enacted, etc., as follows: —

SECTION 1. From and after the first day of July, in the year eighteen hundred and sixty-eight, no house, building, or portion thereof, in the City of Boston, then used, occupied, leased, or rented for a tenement or lodging house, shall continue to be so used, occupied, leased, or rented, unless the same, on the requisition of the Board of Health, shall conform in its construction and appurtenances to the provisions of this act.

SECT. 2. Every house, building, or portion thereof, in the City of Boston, designed to be used, occupied, leased, or rented, or which is used, occupied, leased, or rented for a tenement or lodging house, shall have in every room which is occupied as a sleeping-room, and which does not communicate directly with the external air, a ventilating or transom window, having an opening or area of three square feet, over the door leading into and connected with the adjoining room, if such adjoining room communicates with the external air; and also a ventilating or transom window, of the same opening or area, communicating with the entry or hall of the house, or where this is, from the relative situations of the rooms, impracticable, such last-mentioned ventilating or transom window shall communicate with an adjoining room that itself communicates with the entry or hall. Every such house or building shall have in the roof, at the top of the hall, an adequate and proper ventilator, of a form approved by the Board of Health or the superintendent.

SECT. 3. *Every such house shall be provided with a proper fire-escape, or means of escape in case of fire, to be approved by the superintendent of the Board of Health.*

SECT. 4. The roof of every such house shall be kept in good repair and so as not to leak, and all rain-water shall be so drained or conveyed therefrom as to prevent its dripping on the ground or causing dampness in the walls, yard, or area. All stairs shall be provided with proper balusters or railings, and shall be kept in good repair.

SECT. 5. Every such building shall be provided with good and sufficient water-closets or privies, of a construction approved by the Board of Health, and shall have proper doors, traps, soil-pans, and other suitable works and arrangements so far as may be necessary to insure the efficient operation thereof. Such water-closets or privies shall not be less in number than one to every twenty occupants of said house; but water-closets and privies may be used in common by the occupants of any two or more houses: *provided*, the access is convenient and direct; and *provided*, the number of occupants in the houses for which they are provided shall not exceed the proportion above required for every privy or water-closet. Every such house situated upon a lot on a street in which there is a sewer, shall have the water-closets or privies furnished with a proper connection with the sewer, which connection shall be in all its parts adequate for the purpose, so as to permit entirely and freely to pass whatever enters the same. Such connection with the sewer shall be of a form approved by the Board of Health or superintendent, and all such water-closets and vaults shall be provided with the proper traps, and connected with the house-sewer by a proper tight pipe, and shall be provided with sufficient water and other proper means of flushing the same; and every owner, lessee, and occupant shall take due measures to prevent improper substances from entering such water-closets or privies or their connections, and to secure the prompt removal of any improper substances that may enter them, so that no accumulation shall take place, and so as to prevent any exhalations therefrom, offensive, dangerous, or prejudicial to life or health, and so as to prevent the same from being or becoming obstructed. No cesspool shall be allowed in or under or connected with any such house, except when it is unavoidable, and in such case it shall be constructed in such situation and in such manner as the Board of Health or superintendent may direct. It shall in all cases be water-tight, and arched or securely covered over, and no offensive smell or gases shall be allowed to escape therefrom, or from any privy or privy vault. In all cases where a sewer exists in the street upon which the house or building stands, the yard or area shall be so connected with the same that all water, from the roof or otherwise, and all liquid filth shall pass freely into it. Where no sewer exists in the street, the yard or area shall be so graded that all water, from the roof or otherwise, and all filth shall flow freely from it and all parts of it into the street gutter, by a passage beneath the sidewalk, which shall be covered by a permanent cover, but so arranged as to permit access to remove obstructions or impurities.

SECT. 6. From and after the first day of July, in the year eighteen hundred and sixty-eight, it shall not be lawful, without a permit from the Board of Health or superintendent, to let or occupy or suffer to be occupied separately as a dwelling, any vault, cellar, or underground room, built or rebuilt after said date, or which shall not have been so let or occupied before said date. And from and after the first day of July, in the year eighteen hundred and sixty-nine, it shall not be lawful, without such permit, to let or continue to be let, or to occupy or suffer to be occupied, separately as a dwelling, any vault, cellar, or underground room whatsoever, unless the same be in every part thereof at least seven feet in height, measured from the floor to the ceiling thereof, nor unless the same be for at least one foot of its height above the surface of the street or ground adjoining or nearest to the same, nor unless there be outside of and adjoining the said vault, cellar, or room, and extending along the entire frontage thereof, and upwards from six inches below the level of the floor thereof up to the surface of the said street or ground, an open space of at least two feet and six inches wide in every part, nor unless the same be well and effectually drained by means of a drain, the uppermost part of which is one foot at least below the level of the floor of such vault, cellar, or room, nor unless there is a clear space of not less than one foot below the level of the floor, except where the same is cemented, nor unless there be appurtenant to such vault, cellar, or room the use of a water-closet or privy, kept and provided as in this act required, nor unless the same have an external window-opening of at least nine superficial feet clear of the sash-frame, in which window-opening there shall be fitted a frame filled in with glazed sashes, at least four and a half superficial feet of which shall be made so as to open for the purpose of ventilation: *provided, however,* that in case of an inner or back vault, cellar, or room, let or occupied along with a front vault, cellar, or room as part of the same letting or occupation, it shall be a sufficient compliance with the provisions of this act, if the front room is provided with a window as hereinbefore provided, and if the said back vault, cellar, or room is connected with the front vault, cellar, or room by a door, and also by a proper ventilating or transom window, and where practicable, also connected by a proper ventilating or transom window, or by some hall or passage, or with the external air: *provided, always,* that in any area adjoining a vault, cellar, or underground room, there may be steps necessary for access to such vault, cellar, or room, if the same be so placed as not to be over, across, or opposite to said external window, and so as to allow between every part of such steps and the external wall of such vault, cellar, or room, a clear space of six inches at least, and if the rise of said steps is open; and, *provided, further,* that over or across any such area there may be steps necessary for access to any building above the vault, cellar, or room to which such area adjoins, if the same be so placed as not to be over, across, or opposite to any such external window.

SECT. 7. *From and after the first day of July, in the year eighteen hundred and sixty-eight, no vault, cellar, or underground room in any tenement or lodging house shall be occupied as a place of lodging or sleeping, except the same shall be approved in writing, and a permit given therefor by the Board of Health or superintendent.*

SECT. 8. *Every tenement or lodging house shall have the proper and suitable conveniences or receptacles for receiving garbage and other refuse matters. No tenement or lodging house, or any portion thereof, shall be used as a place of storage for any combustible article, or any article dangerous to life or detrimental to health; nor shall any horse, cow, calf, swine, pig, sheep, or goat be kept in said house.*

SECT. 9. *Every tenement or lodging house, and every part thereof, shall be kept clean and free from any accumulation of dirt, filth, garbage, or other matter in or on the same, or in the yard, court, passage, area, or alley connected with or belonging to the same. The owner or keeper of any lodging-house, and the owner or lessee of any tenement-house or part thereof, shall thoroughly cleanse all the rooms, passages, stairs, floors, windows, doors, walls, ceilings, privies, cesspools and drains thereof of the house or part of the house of which he is the owner or lessee, to the satisfaction of the Board of Health, so often as shall be required by or in accord-*

ance with any regulation or ordinance of said city, and shall well and sufficiently, to the satisfaction of said Board, whitewash the walls and ceilings thereof twice at least in every year, in the months of April and October, unless the said Board shall otherwise direct. Every tenement or lodging house shall have legibly posted or painted on the wall or door in the entry, or some public accessible place, the name and address of the owner or owners, and of the agent or agents, or any one having charge of the renting and collecting of the rents for the same; and service of any papers required by this act, or by any proceedings to enforce any of its provisions, or of the acts relating to the Board of Health, shall be sufficient if made upon the person or persons so designated as owner or owners, agent or agents.

SECT. 10. *The keeper of any lodging-house and the owner, agent of the owner, lessee, and occupant of any tenement-house, and every other person having the care or management thereof, shall at all times, when required by any officer of the Board of Health, or by any officer upon whom any duty or authority is conferred by this act, give him free access to such house and to every part thereof.* The owner or keeper of any lodging-house, and the owner, agent of the owner, and the lessee of any tenement-house or part thereof shall, whenever any person in such house is sick of fever, or of any infectious, pestilential, or contagious disease, and such sickness is known to such owner, keeper, agent, or lessee, give immediate notice thereof to the Board of Health, or to some officer of the same, and, thereupon, said Board shall cause the same to be inspected, and may, if found necessary, cause the same to be immediately cleansed or disinfected at the expense of the owner, in such manner as they may deem necessary and effectual; and they may also cause the blankets, bedding, and bedclothes used by any such sick person, to be thoroughly cleansed, scoured, and fumigated, and in extreme cases to be destroyed.

SECT. 11. Whenever it shall be certified to the Board of Health by the superintendent that any building or part thereof is unfit for human habitation, by reason of its being so infected with disease as to be likely to cause sickness among the occupants, or by reason of its want of repair has become dangerous to life, said Board may issue an order, and cause the same to be affixed conspicuously on the building or part thereof, and to be personally served upon the owner, agent, or lessee, if the same can be found in this State, requiring all persons therein to vacate such building, for the reasons to be stated therein as aforesaid. Such building or part thereof shall, within ten days thereafter, be vacated or within such shorter time, not less than twenty-four hours, as in said notice may be specified; but said Board, if it shall become satisfied that the danger from said house or part thereof has ceased to exist, may revoke said order, and it shall thenceforward become inoperative.

SECT. 12. No house hereafter erected shall be used as a tenement-house or lodging-house, and no house heretofore erected, and not now used for such purpose, shall be converted into, used or leased for a tenement or lodging house, unless, in addition to the requirements hereinbefore contained, it conforms to the requirements contained in the following sections.

SECT. 13. It shall not be lawful hereafter to erect for or convert to the purposes of a tenement or lodging house a building on the front of any lot where there is another building on the rear of the same lot, unless there is a clear, open space, exclusively belonging to the front building and extending upwards from the ground, of at least ten feet, between said buildings, if they are one story high, above the level of the ground; if they are two stories high, the distance between them shall not be less than fifteen feet; if they are three stories high, the distance between them shall be twenty feet; and if they are more than three stories high, the distance between them shall be twenty-five feet. At the rear of every building hereafter erected for or converted to the purposes of a tenement or lodging house on the back part of any lot, there shall be a clear, open space of ten feet between it and any other building. But when thorough ventilation of such open spaces can be otherwise secured, said distances may be lessened or modified, in special cases, by a permit from the Board of Health or the superintendent.

SECT. 14. In every such house hereafter erected or converted every habitable room, except rooms in the attic, shall be in every part not less than eight feet in height from the floor to the ceiling; and every habitable room in the attic of any such building shall be at least eight feet in height from the floor to the ceiling, throughout not less than one half the area of such room. Every such room shall have at least one window connecting with the external air, or over the door a suitable ventilator, connecting it with a room or hall which has a connection with the external air. The total area of window in every room communicating with the external air, shall be equal to at least one tenth of the superficial area of every such room; and the top of one, at least, of such windows shall not be less than seven feet and six inches above the floor, and the upper half of each window shall be so made as to open for the purposes of ventilation. Every habitable room of a less area than one hundred superficial feet, if it does not communicate directly with the external air, and is without an open fireplace, shall be provided with special means of ventilation by a separate air-shaft extending to the roof, or otherwise, as the Board of Health may prescribe.

SECT. 15. *Every such house hereafter erected or converted, shall have adequate chimneys running through every floor, with an open fireplace or grate, or place for a stove, properly connected with one of said chimneys, for every family and set of apartments. It shall have proper conveniences and receptacles or ashes and rubbish; it shall have water furnished at one or more places in such house, or in the yard thereof, so that the same may be adequate and reasonably convenient for the use of the occupants thereof. It shall have the floor of the cellar properly cemented, so as to be water-tight. The halls on each floor shall open directly to the external air, with suitable windows, and shall have no room or other obstruction at the end, unless sufficient light or ventilation is otherwise provided for said halls, in a manner approved by the Board or the superintendent.*

SECT. 16. Every owner or other person violating any provision of this act, after the same shall take effect, shall be guilty of a misdemeanor, punishable by a fine not exceeding one hundred dollars, or by imprisonment not exceeding sixty days.

SECT. 17. *A tenement-house within the meaning of this act, shall be taken to mean and include every house, building, or portion thereof which is rented, leased, let, or hired out to be occupied, or is occupied, as the house or residence of more than three families living independently of another, and doing their cooking upon the premises, or by more than two families upon a floor, so living and cooking, but having a common right in the halls, stairways, yards, water-closets, or privies, or some of them.*

A lodging-house shall be taken to mean and include any house or building, or portion thereof, in which persons are lodged for hire for a single night, or for less than a week at one time.

A cellar shall be taken to mean and include every basement or lower story of any building or house, of which one half or more of the height from the floor to the ceiling is below the level of the street adjoining.

SECT. 18. The Board of Health shall have authority to make other regulations as to cellars and as to ventilation, consistent with the foregoing, where it shall be satisfied that such regulations will secure equally well the health of the occupants. All complaints under this act shall be made only by authority of the Board of Health, and the Municipal Court of the City of Boston shall have jurisdiction concurrent with the Superior Court of all offences against the provisions of this act. [*Approved June* 4, 1868.

THE END.

Cambridge : Stereotyped and Printed by Welch, Bigelow, & Co.

www.ingramcontent.com/pod-product-compliance
Lightning Source LLC
LaVergne TN
LVHW011204110826
845150LV00006B/1321